Ed Glinert

111 Places in London's East End That You Shouldn't Miss

Photographs by Marc Zakian

T0346460

emons:

For Katy

© Emons Verlag GmbH
All rights reserved
© Photographs by Marc Zakian
© Cover motif: shutterstock.com/Phant
Edited by Rosalind Horton
Layout: Eva Kraskes, based on a design
by Lübbeke | Naumann | Thoben
Maps: altancicek.design, www.altancicek.de
Basic cartographical information from Openstreetmap,
© OpenStreetMap-Mitwirkende, ODbL
Printing and binding: CPI – Clausen & Bosse, Leck
Printed in Germany 2020
ISBN 978-3-7408-0752-8
First edition

Did you enjoy this guidebook? Would you like to see more?
Join us in uncovering new places around the world on:
www.111places.com

Foreword

'The East End is a vast city … a shocking place … an evil plexus of slums that hide human creeping things; where filthy men and women live on gin, where every citizen wears a black eye.'

Was this written last week? Not quite. That was how journalist Arthur Morrison described the East End in 1894 in his book *Tales of Mean Streets*. Has the East End changed? Well, an area that decent civilised people used to refuse to enter without a police escort is now – horror of horrors – gentrified, sort of. Where there used to be evil pubs full of blokes whose cigarettes pointed inwards to their palm, who the Kray twins feared (you have to go to Romford for that now), there are now funky coffee outlets and quirky shops selling flower pots. Where there used to be gangs behind Bethnal Green Road keen on garrotting strangers, there are now themed cocktail bars and film clubs.

Has this ruined the East End? Not at all. The East End is THE place to go in the capital. Faced with a choice between St Paul's Cathedral, Westminster Abbey and Buckingham Palace, head instead for Narrow Street in Limehouse. That is the essence of London. The land of Dickens' mudlarks, ghosts of explorers heading out to Baffin Island, phantoms of pirates and privateers, stevedores and sailmakers, ships bringing in tea, rum, coffee and tobacco from the Indies. And the East End can even boast of Britain's favourite tourist attraction: The Tower of London.

Where is the East End? To those who like to get things pedantically correct it is simply E1, E2, E3 and E14. Away from the numbers, that means Aldgate, Bethnal Green, Bow, Bromley-by-Bow, Canary Wharf, Cubitt Town, Limehouse, Mile End, Millwall (yes), Poplar, Ratcliffe, Shadwell, (some of) Shoreditch, Spitalfields, Stepney, Wapping and Whitechapel. Places not in the East End but that cab drivers, football reporters and *Guardian* journalists think are: Dalston, Hackney, Hoxton, West Ham and Southend.

And I haven't even mentioned Jack the Ripper yet.

111 Places

1 Aldgate Pump
Gateway to the East End

Aldgate Pump is the historic entrance to the East End. It is situated at the East End's border with the City of London, at the location where the last wolf was shot locally, which explains the plaque of a wolf's head on the structure.

The pump was built on the site of the ancient Aldgate Well, served from underground streams that are now sewers. It was first recorded in the 16th century and originally stood a few yards away from the current model, to be moved here in the 1870s. Nearby was the original Aldgate – the Old Gate – demolished in 1761, from where distances into Essex were measured and where Geoffrey Chaucer worked as a customs official in rooms above the gate from 1374 to 1386.

Although the pump no longer expels water, it retains an infamous place in local history. In 1876 several hundred people died in the 'Aldgate Pump epidemic' after taking the waters. So much for an earlier description of their quality as 'bright, sparkling, and cool, and of an agreeable taste.' The pleasant taste came from calcium in the water, and the calcium came from the bones of the dead, the water having run through nearby graveyards. By the 1920s this was a distant memory and Whittard's tea merchants used to 'always get the kettles filled at the Aldgate Pump so that only the purest water was used for tea tasting.'

The pump came to be used in the local vernacular and in rhyming slang. A bouncing cheque was known as 'a draught upon Aldgate Pump', and the phrase 'Aldgate Pump' itself stood for 'to get the hump' – to be annoyed. Aldgate Pump was mentioned by Dickens in *The Uncommercial Traveller*: 'My day's business beckoned me to the East End of London; I had turned my face to that part of the compass … and had got past Aldgate Pump.' However, an anonymous contemporary author noted how 'east of Aldgate Pump people cared for nothing but drink, vice and crime.'

Address Junction of Leadenhall Street, Fenchurch Street and Aldgate High Street, EC3A 2DX | Getting there Underground to Aldgate (Circle and Metropolitan lines) | Hours Accessible 24 hours | Tip The Aldgate, like all the other six ancient London gates, has long since disappeared. The only landmark in the vicinity, now dominated by finance houses, that has survived modern-day redevelopment is the 1740s' tower of St Botolph's Church by George Dance the Elder.

2 Ancient Stepney Church
The East End's oldest church

The church of St Dunstan and All Saints stands on the site of the oldest place of worship in the East End. This, the third such church on the site, was built of Kentish ragstone in the 15th century. Details of the first church to stand here are unknown, but in the year 952, Dunstan, the Bishop of London, who had been Abbot of Glastonbury and Archbishop of Canterbury, and was now the Lord of the Manor of Stepney, replaced the existing wooden structure with a stone church dedicated to all the saints. In 1029, Dunstan was canonised and the church rededicated to St Dunstan and All Saints.

When the parish went to appoint Richard Foxe as vicar in 1484, the king, Richard III, objected on the grounds that he was keeping company with the 'great rebel, Henry ap Tuddor,' the eventual Henry VII. After Henry beat off Richard later that year at the Battle of Bosworth, Foxe was rewarded with several major offices, including principal Secretary of State, Lord Privy Seal and Bishop of Exeter.

The carvings in the spandrels of the arch at the entrance of the church are wonderfully informative. On the left is one of a ship in honour of the area's long association with river-borne trade and travel. The church used to fly a flag with a red ensign, the merchant navy symbol, and allow those born at sea to be registered in the parish of Stepney. On the right is a carving of the devil. This refers to the legend of St Dunstan pulling the nose of the devil with red hot tongs. The church bells are mentioned in the nursery rhyme 'Oranges and Lemons' in the lines 'When will that be? say the bells of Stepney.' In the long-abandoned graveyard is the stone of Roger Crab, 17th-century hermit who subsisted on a frugal diet of herbs, roots, leaves, grass and water. The church was lucky to survive a major fire in 1901 that saw headlines such as 'A Stepney Disaster – Parish Church Burnt Down.'

Address Off Stepney High Street, east of the eastern end of Stepney Way, E1 0NR |
Getting there Limehouse National Rail station | **Hours** Intermittent during the week, plus
Sunday morning | **Tip** Stepney Way, which stretches out from the western end of the church
grounds, is an ancient route towards London that was part of an equally ancient parish in
the Ossulstone, an obsolete subdivision or hundred of Middlesex, the county that covered
much of London until 1965.

3 Aquatics Centre

One of so many new treasures in Stratford Olympia

People will long argue over whether it was worth bulldozing the railway sidings and 1930s' industrial units of Stratford to build a monumental new city – a living theme park as some have called it – around the excuse of the 2012 Olympic Games. The PR people are convinced, touting Queen Elizabeth Park as 'Here East: a world-leading creative and digital cluster and London's home for making.' That translates as saying the area is full of amenities, creating a greater legacy than similar recent projects in Athens and Beijing, and one of the most popular and best used new ventures is the Aquatics Centre.

The Aquatics Centre is located appropriately by the Waterworks River, which had to be moved, and unearthed four skeletons from a prehistoric settlement. This is *the* place for swimming. Inside are two 50-metre pools and a 25-metre diving pool. Both have moveable floors, so that the depth can be changed. The complex was designed by the flamboyant Iraqi architect Zaha Hadid who had recently won the Pritzker Prize, the most prestigious in architecture. Hadid was inspired by the idea of 'moving water'; the exterior looks like a whale. The IOC President Jacques Rogge described the Centre as a 'masterpiece', but costs inevitably fell off the deep end and rose to £240 million.

The venue featured 32 events during the Games, which saw the United States win 31 medals. Michael Phelps secured his status as the most decorated Olympian of all time, winning six medals and ending his Olympic career here. The British team also prospered. Michael Jamieson won a silver medal in the 200-metre breaststroke, and Rebecca Adlington bronze medals in the 400-metre and 800-metre freestyle events. Tom Daley took a bronze diving from the 10-metre platform. After the Olympics, the Centre was remodelled and reopened as a public amenity in March 2014. And so a new Stratford continues to thrive.

Address Queen Elizabeth Olympic Park, Stratford E20 2AQ | Getting there Underground to Stratford (Central and Jubilee lines), DLR, Overground & National Rail | Hours Daily 6am–10.30pm | Tip Leave the water to explore the waterside of a bewildering array of rivers and tributaries of the River Lea in this area, best equipped with an old OS map to see how the waterways have been moved.

4 — ArcelorMittal *Orbit*
Crazy name, crazy sculpture

This barely believable, unfeasibly monstrous, over 90-metre high, £23-million tower in the new Queen Elizabeth Park is the UK's biggest piece of public art.

The Independent described *Orbit* as 'a continuously looping lattice made up of eight strands winding into each other and combined by rings like a jagged knot.' It was devised as part of the huge overhaul of the East End edgelands in time for the 2012 Olympics, for which it will be a permanent legacy. The structure incorporates the world's tallest and longest tunnel slide at 177 metres.

The designers were led by the Turner Prize-winning artist Anish Kapoor. The impetus came from politicians Boris Johnson and Tessa Jowell who believed the Olympic site needed 'something extra, stunning, ambitious … world-class art in the Olympic Park to distinguish the east London skyline and arouse the curiosity and wonder of Londoners and visitors' – even to rival the Eiffel Tower or Statue of Liberty. In the face of potential criticism Johnson noted: 'Of course some people will say we are nuts – in the depths of a recession – to be building Britain's biggest ever piece of public art, but I am certain that this is the right thing for the site.'

Designs that were discarded included a 119-metre steel colossus, *Olympian Man*, by Antony Gormley and Paul Fryer's *Transmission*, a 122-metre structure resembling a cross between a pylon and a Native American totem pole. Of the £22-million-plus cost, £16 million came from steel tycoon Lakshmi Mittal, then Britain's richest man. Mittal's involvement stemmed from a chance meeting with Boris Johnson in a cloakroom in Davos in January 2009. The Tory politician put the idea to Mittal, who immediately agreed to supply the steel. Later Mittal explained that he never expected it was going to be such a huge project. He thought he would simply be supplying some steel.

Address Queen Elizabeth Olympic Park, E20 2AD | Getting there Underground
to Stratford (Central and Jubilee lines), Overground to Stratford or Hackney Wick;
bus D8 or 339 | Hours Mon–Fri 11am–4pm, Sat & Sun 10am–6pm; the slide will open
30 minutes after the attraction opens | Tip The structure stands in between two branches
of the River Lea, the City Mill River and the Waterworks River. The Lea is the ancient
boundary between the East End and Essex, and it splits up at this point into what could be
called the Lea delta, with the Three Mills River, Bow Back River and Channelsea River all
flowing in the vicinity.

5 Arnold Circus Bandstand
A reminder of early 20th-century civic progress

The only surviving bandstand in the East End sits atop a raised mound made from the rubble left over when London's worst Victorian slum, the Old Nichol, was levelled early in the 20th century. Nowadays, six roads radiate from Arnold Circus to what is an interesting mix of ultra-chic hipster shops on Redchurch Street and Bangladeshi council flats in the Boundary Estate, which was the country's first council estate when it opened in 1900.

At least the Old Nichol has gone. In a 19th-century London filled with hellholes and no-go zones – Saffron Hill, Seven Dials, Whitechapel – the Old Nichol was particularly horrid. To the East End novelist Arthur Morrison it was 'the blackest pit in London,' while the *Illustrated London News* damned the place as 'a neighbourhood as foul as can be discovered in the civilised world, [its] population, huddled in dark cellars, ruined garrets, bare and blackened rooms, teeming with disease and death, depressed almost to the last stage of human endurance.'

The local diet consisted mostly of offal: cow-heels, bullocks' hearts, kidneys, livers, tripe and sheep's heads. An 1848 survey of the housing found dwellings 'constructed in defiance of every law and principle on which the health and lives of the occupants depend.' All around were rubbish tips made of dung, decomposing vegetables and animal remains. The death rate was four times the national average. The Old Nichol even had the worst crime rate in London – and some of the worst stories. In 1831, two local men, John Bishop and Thomas Head, abducted Carlo Ferrari, a 14-year-old Italian boy, drugged him with rum laced with laudanum, and then drowned him in a nearby well. When Bishop and Head tried to sell the body to surgeons at King's College, the police were called. They arrested the pair, who were convicted and hanged at Newgate in front of a crowd of 30,000 people.

Address Arnold Circus, Shoreditch E2 7JS | Getting there Overground to Shoreditch High Street; bus 388 | Hours Accessible 24 hours | Tip Club Row, which leads south from Arnold Circus, was where exotic animals were sold, particularly on Sunday mornings, until European legislation clamped down on the practice in the 1970s.

6 _ Banglatown
Brick Lane and the Bangladeshi immigration

The streets around Brick Lane have witnessed one of the biggest demographic upheavals in London history in recent years. What was for a hundred years a Jewish ghetto has become a major centre for Asian immigration, marked with the Banglatown arch at the southern end of Brick Lane. The arch is not just a testament to the new residents, it is also an act of defiance, to cement the pride of the locals in combating years of violent opposition.

The first arrivals from East India in the 1970s were mostly men who had jumped ship or been left stranded at the dockside, with no passage home for weeks. There were only two local properties that welcomed them. Soon they were joined by large numbers of Bengalis fleeing the harshness of life in humid, rainy, impoverished, overcrowded Bangladesh and moving here. To help find their way around the East End they left bricks along the pavements to mark the route. They adopted pictorial codes to remember the bus routes: two eggs for the no. 8 to Oxford Street, two hooks for the no. 22 to Piccadilly Circus.

Bangladeshis joined the local textile industry, one of the few professions open to them. Initially this meant Bangladeshi women buttonholing, cutting and trimming in poor light with out-of-date hazardous machines. Eventually the new immigrants created a new mass local industry: the curry house. The downside was assaults on Bangladeshis perpetuated by skinheads and the quasi-fascist National Front. This culminated in the murder of Altab Ali who was chased along Brick Lane and stabbed to death near Aldgate East station on 4 May, 1978. Seven thousand Bangladeshis marched to Downing Street behind Ali's coffin. Revival was championed by a visit from President Ziaur Rahman of Bangladesh who took a street sign back to Dacca to rename a street there Brick Lane. From the 1980s, racism gradually abated as the area became almost entirely Asian.

Address Brick Lane, just north of Wentworth Street junction, E1 6PU | Getting there Underground to Aldgate East (District and Hammersmith & City lines); bus 8 or 388 | Hours Accessible 24 hours | Tip A quarter of a mile south-east of the arch, on Whitechapel Road, is a small green space left over when the church of St Mary Matfelon that gave Whitechapel its name was destroyed in World War II. It has been named Altab Ali Park after the Bangladeshi youth murdered in 1978.

7 Beigel Bake

Legendary 24-7 Jewish café

The queues stretch out into the road at what is the most famous and sought after take-away in London, let alone the East End. The service is lightning quick, the prices absurdly cheap, and the shop is open all day, all night, all year.

Beigel Bake opened in 1974 when the area still had a Jewish community. The food is in the traditional north European Jewish style, dominated by beigels stuffed with smoked salmon and cream cheese, or what is now almost impossible to find in the capital: authentic salt beef, the portions so vast they fall out of the sandwich. The shop produces some 7,000 beigels a day. There are no tables or chairs for customers, just a long counter along one tiled wall, inviting a quick turnaround. The art of making the beigel is a closely guarded secret, although it can be revealed that the dough is boiled before finally being baked. And watch the beigel maker explain to gullible children how the hole is the most important part.

Despite the culinary euphoria, the establishment was involved in a terrible tragedy recently. In August 2017 two members of the owners' family, Leah Cohen, and her daughter, Hannah, were found stabbed to death in the family home in Golders Green. Astonishingly, the culprit was Leah's son, Joshua Cohen, 27, who had discovered he had been cut out of the family's baking fortune only weeks earlier. He was arrested in nearby Golders Hill Park the following day and charged with two counts of murder.

Joshua's late father, Asher, was one of the founders of the shop. When probate was granted on his estate, it named only Cohen's two older brothers, Nathan, 30, and Daniel, 34, as directors of the company. The judge ruled Joshua unfit to stand trial as he was suffering from paranoid schizophrenia 'characterised by thought disorder and paranoid delusions.' He has since been incarcerated at Broadmoor high-security hospital.

Address 159 Brick Lane, Spitalfields E1 6SB | Getting there Overground to Shoreditch High Street | Hours Open 24 hours | Tip Brick Lane is as equally well known for its myriad curry houses that stretch the entire length of the street, outside which hopeful staff implore passers-by to try theirs and theirs only.

8 Ben Truman Chimney

When this brewery ruled the ale world

Towering over Brick Lane is the lofty Ben Truman chimney, a reminder of the days when this complex housed the biggest brewery in the world. Although no beer has been brewed here this century, the sprawling buildings have been wonderfully preserved and are now home to myriad stalls, workshops, studios, media company offices, furniture showrooms and food outlets.

A Thomas Bucknall built the Black Eagle brewhouse here in 1666, the year of the Great Fire of London. Joseph Truman acquired the brewery in 1679. His son, Benjamin, became so powerful he was able to loan money to the Crown to finance the country's wars. Thomas Gainsborough even painted his portrait in one of his largest canvasses.

Ben Truman brewed a drink that came to be known as porter, thanks to its popularity with the porters of London. The air was filled with the smell of hops and yeast, and workers were welcomed each morning with their own pewter jug that would be filled with two pints of ale. Porter became the first beer to be mass produced, but its popularity was later supplanted by pale ale. Ben Truman's ales went on to receive the royal blessing, despite an unfortunate incident when the Duchess of Brunswick, a granddaughter of George II, was born in 1737. A barrel ordered by the royal household was found to be of such poor quality revellers threw the beer in each other's faces and the barrels into the fire. Fortunately for the brewery, the Prince ordered another barrel for the following night 'with which the populace was pleased and satisfied.'

In the 19th century, Truman's became Truman, Hanbury and Buxton, and their motifs can still be seen on pub walls throughout the East End. Ben Truman's brand failed to meet the challenges of the push for 'real ale' in the 1970s. The brewery closed in the 1980s, but the brand was revived in 2010 and is now brewed just outside the East End in Hackney Wick.

Address 91 Brick Lane, Spitalfields E1 6QR | Getting there Overground to Shoreditch High Street | Hours Accessible 24 hours | Tip Brick Lane now has no pubs, something unthinkable a few generations ago. Yet many of the pub buildings remain, having been converted into curry houses and coffee houses. The nearest pub, just off Brick Lane at 3 Heneage Street, is The Pride of Spitalfields, a throwback to the days of proper pubs.

9 Bethnal Green Tube Station Disaster Memorial

Stairway to heaven replaces stairway to death

The biggest civilian loss of life during World War II occurred at Bethnal Green tube station on 3 March, 1943. The station was not then in use, as it was the first stop on a new extension of the Central Line east of Liverpool Street, but it had been turned into a major air-raid shelter, with more than 5,000 bunk beds and room for 5,000 more people in makeshift set-ups. Unfortunately, entrance was through only one narrow opening, which led to a staircase lit by a single 25-watt bulb, the steps wet from rain.

By the beginning of 1943 the worst raids seemed to be over, and only some 250 people were using the Bethnal Green shelter most nights. However, early in March there was a raid on Berlin and the War Office was expecting reprisals. The night before the disaster some 850 people used the shelter. At 8pm on the night of 3 March an air-raid warning sounded and hundreds made for the station. Then came a thunderous sound from the park. People in their panic mused what it could be. Bombs didn't have that type of sound. Perhaps it was land mines? It was a new type of anti-aircraft salvo, and it led to a stampede at the top of the station, while at the bottom of the steps a girl stumbled. Someone fell on top of her, and someone else on top of them. People at the top pushed, exacerbating the crush at the bottom. One hundred and seventy-eight people died, 62 of them children, mostly suffocating. A further 62 were seriously injured.

The government suppressed news of the disaster. Neither the place nor the number of casualties was mentioned in the press. Nazi radio boasted of panic in London from German bombs, the news conveyed to them by fifth columnists in the British Union of Fascists who, ironically, were based in Bethnal Green.

Address Top of the south-east entrance to Bethnal Green tube station, west end of Roman Road, Bethnal Green E2 0ET | Getting there Underground to Bethnal Green (Central line); bus 8, 106, 254, 309 or 388 | Hours Accessible 24 hours | Tip At the same junction stands the Salmon and Ball pub, a regular meeting place for the British Union of Fascists in the 1930s. Their HQ, a cowshed just off the Bethnal Green Road, was demolished only as recently as 2016.

10 Billingsgate Market
The carp and sole of the fish world

After centuries of being set by the Tower and the Thames, Billingsgate now occupies this huge site, developed with the very latest technology, at the north end of the Isle of Dogs. A building that was erected in 1982, the market complex covers an area of 13 acres. The ground floor consists of a large trading hall with 98 stands and 30 shops, 2 cafés, cold rooms, a 1,500-tonne freezer, an ice-making plant, and 14 lock-up shops used mainly by catering suppliers and assorted merchants.

Each trading day offers buyers the largest selection of fish in the United Kingdom, thanks to daily arrivals from the coast by road from ports as far afield as Aberdeen and Cornwall. With around 40 merchants trading in close proximity, competition is fierce. There's even a training school at Billingsgate supported by the City of London Corporation and the Worshipful Company of Fishmongers aimed at encouraging young people to enjoy seafood as part of a healthy diet, established at a time when obesity levels began to soar and fish consumption was on the decline.

Billingsgate was established formally by an Act of Parliament in 1699. By the mid-19th century it consisted only of shed buildings by Billingsgate Dock, with a range of wooden houses and little shelter until successive extensions and improvements. Boats delivered fish to a small inlet of the Thames and business took place on the quayside. The City of London Corporation still runs the market and pays an annual ground rent, stipulated in an agreement between the latter and Tower Hamlets Council, of 'the gift of one fish.' Past workers here include the Kray twins. Reggie worked as a salesman while Ronnie's job was collecting empty fish boxes.

The traders still use the infamously coarse curses that once made the word 'Billingsgate' a byword for crude and vulgar language, as used historically by 'fishwives'.

Address Trafalgar Way, Poplar E14 5ST | Getting there Underground to Canary Wharf (Jubilee line); Overground to Canary Wharf Crossrail | Hours Tue–Sat 5–8.30am, closed Tuesdays following a Bank Holiday Monday | Tip If you can't manage Billingsgate's extraordinarily early hours, there's always Ernie's Snack Bar, a small white van, dispensing food and drink to the office and construction workers, tucked away behind offices off Marsh Wall. Ernie Bennett who began the venture was Canary Wharf's first retailer when Olympia & York started the Canary Wharf development.

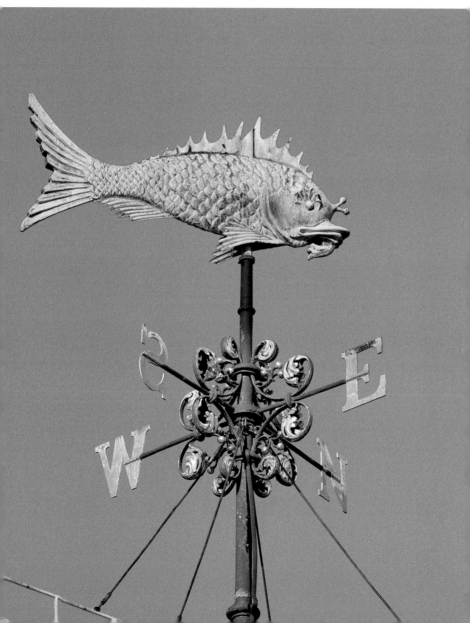

11 The Blind Beggar

The East End's most infamous gangster pub

The most infamous gangland killing in East End history took place inside this popular pub on the evening of 9 March, 1966 when Ronnie Kray shot dead fellow gangster George Cornell. His victim was a member of the rival Richardson gang who was taking a chance venturing north of the river. 'Taking a liberty,' as Kray put it.

Cornell was supping a light ale at the bar when in walked the notorious younger Kray twin with an accomplice, 'Scotch' Ian Barrie. Their driver, John Dickson, was waiting outside in a Mark 1 Cortina. Cornell exclaimed what were to be his last words, 'Well, look who's here then?', and after Ian Barrie fired into the ceiling Kray aimed his 9mm Mauser between Cornell's eyes and shot him dead. The needle of the record player, which was playing the Walker Brothers' song 'The Sun Ain't Gonna Shine Anymore' at the time, stuck on the word 'anymore,' which it began to play repeatedly.

Ronnie's excuse for the murder was that Cornell, in front of witnesses, had called him a 'fat poof … he virtually signed his own death warrant.' After the shooting, the Kray entourage quickly headed out of the East End to the Chequers pub on High Street Walthamstow. Years later, the pistol was found in the mud of the River Lea and is now in Scotland Yard's Black Museum.

Kray was so convinced he was untouchable he returned to the pub often to order a 'luger and lime'. The East End gangland code of *omertà* meant that 'nobody in the pub saw nuffink'; not Albie Woods and Johnny Dale who were at one end of the bar, nor a 79-year-old man at the other end reading a newspaper, nor the barmaid. It took three years to convict Ronnie Kray who, like his brother, Reggie, never left prison again.

The pub is named after Henry de Montfort, son of Simon de Montfort, 6th Earl of Leicester, who posed as a blind beggar after the Battle of Evesham in 1265 to evade detection.

Address 337 Whitechapel Road, Whitechapel E1 1BU, +44 (0)207 247 6195 | **Getting there** Underground (District and Hammersmith & City lines) or Overground to Whitechapel | **Hours** Sun–Thu 11am–11pm, Fri & Sat 11am–midnight | **Tip** Other nearby pubs associated with the Krays and their ilk have long since closed as pubs, though the buildings remain. These include the Grave Maurice at 269 Whitechapel Road, now a shop, and the Lord Rodney's Head at no. 285, now a curry house.

12 Bloody Tower

Where the Princes in the Tower were murdered

The Bloody Tower is one of 21 towers in the Tower of London, one of the world's most visited attractions. It is known as the Bloody Tower on account of the amount of blood that has been spilled here over the centuries. The Bloody Tower was built in the 1220s as the Garden Tower, and its upper storey opened onto a parade ground that had been the Constable's garden. Its purpose was to control the main river entrance to the buildings.

Here in the summer of 1483, in one of the most infamous murders in English history, Edward V and his brother, Richard Duke of York, the Princes in the Tower, were slain by an unknown assailant, popularly believed to be in the pay of their uncle, Richard Duke of Gloucester, later Richard III.

Some historians believe casting Richard III as villain was Tudor propaganda; that his successor, Henry Tudor, who defeated Richard at the Battle of Bosworth Field in 1485, also had cause to eliminate the two boys. In 1674, bones were discovered in a staircase leading to the White Tower. To add to the macabre history, Henry Percy, 8th Earl of Northumberland, was found dead in his bed here, shot through the heart, on 21 June, 1585. A jury ruled he had committed suicide.

The Bloody Tower's most famous prisoner was Walter Raleigh. He was incarcerated here on 14 July, 1603 by the new king, James I, for his part in a conspiracy to put Lady Arabella Stuart on the throne. As a VIP prisoner, Raleigh was allowed three servants and could use the Lieutenant's garden, where he attempted to grow tobacco. He tried to commit suicide with a table knife. On 17 November, 1603 Raleigh was condemned to death, but the sentence was revoked to life imprisonment. In 1618 he was executed at Westminster. George Jeffreys, the 'Hanging Judge', died in the Bloody Tower in 1688. He had been placed here for his own safety, having sentenced 320 people to be executed.

Address Tower of London, EC3N 4AB, www.hrp.org.uk | **Getting there** Underground to Tower Hill (Circle and District lines); bus 15 | **Hours** Summer (1 Mar–31 Oct) Tue–Sat 9am–5.30pm, Sun & Mon 10am–5.30pm; winter (1 Nov–28 Feb, except 24–26 Dec and 1 Jan) Tue–Sat 9am–4.30pm, Sun & Mon 10am–4.30pm | **Tip** The many towers include the White Tower, the oldest, built in the late 11th century by William the Conqueror; the Wakefield Tower, where Henry VI was murdered in 1471; and the Martin Tower where Colonel Thomas Blood tried to steal the Crown Jewels.

13 Boxpark Shoreditch

Unusual structure for a thriving pop-up centre

At the western end of Bethnal Green Road stands a remarkable and most unusual shopping and leisure centre built from shipping containers. Boxpark described itself as the 'world's first pop-up mall' when it was launched in 2011. It contains more than 60 carefully chosen fashion, arts and lifestyle brands, galleries and cafés, with local names alongside world-famous logos. It describes itself as a 'living, fertile community packed with talent, innovation and attitude' and fills a site that for decades housed an array of labyrinthine curiosity shops built into the now demolished redundant railway arches of the Bishopsgate Goods Yard. In essence it is the hipster version of the glam up-market shopping experience of Westfield by the Olympic Park at the other end of the East End.

The shipping containers were stripped and refitted, painted black and arranged into a small village of retail outlets. Brands were then picked out to inhabit the units. Although on one hand Boxpark nurtures the smaller, edgy and innovative brands, there are units inhabited by the likes of Nike, Calvin Klein and Levi's. However, Boxpark also offers cheap and short-term rents to help young companies get a foothold in an area where prices have been rocketing.

Once it had opened, the upper deck was renovated to cater for street food. Here can be found Pieminister, Rudie's Jerk Shack and the pizza outlet Voodoo Ray's, named after the groundbreaking cult electro number 'Voodoo Ray' by A Guy Called Gerald.

The brains behind the venture was Roger Wade who started out with the street fashion shop Boxfresh. He got the idea in 1999 attending German trade shows. At each show he had to create a mini-shop that was later demolished. This got him thinking about building a trade show stand in a container that could be reused. So successful was Boxpark that others have opened in Croydon and Wembley.

Address 2–10 Bethnal Green Road, Shoreditch E1 6GY, www.boxpark.co.uk | Getting there Overground to Shoreditch High Street | Hours Daily 11am–11pm | Tip To the north on the other side of Bethnal Green Road is Redchurch Street where a similar vibe operates at old-fashioned brick one-storey street level and especially engaging is Labour and Wait (no. 85), founded as an antidote to trend-driven consumerism, the items timeless and functional.

14 Brick Lane

London's hippest street – no contest

Brick Lane is the most exciting street in London, let alone the East End, inheriting the mantle previously worn by Chelsea's King's Road and Regent Street in the West End. Nearly a mile long, stretching south from the hinterland of Bethnal Green almost to Aldgate East station, it is named after the local 16th-century brickworks.

It's the street with everything: a mad manic market, vintage clothes shops, authentically independent coffee houses, ever-changing street art, the best beigel bakery in the world, the biggest conglomeration of curry houses in London, a barber tastelessly called 'Jack the Clipper' (appropriate on the street that might have been the 1756 birthplace of Sweeney Todd, the infamous 'demon barber of Fleet Street') – even a mention in Salman Rushdie's notorious 1988 novel *The Satanic Verses*.

Brick Lane also has a history of conflict and violence. The early 20th-century villain Arthur Harding noted how 'Brick Lane was a hotbed of villainy. Women sold themselves for a few pence. In the back alleys there was garrotting.' Montagu Williams wrote about men 'in a ferocious stage of intoxication' who 'quarrel, fight, and kick, and frenzied women [who fall] upon one another, tearing out hair, scratching, spitting. Verily this is a land flowing with beer and blood.' Perhaps it's best then that Brick Lane nowadays has everything apart from a pub, although the architecture of several buildings reveals Victorian alehouses, and the chimney of the now defunct Ben Truman brewery towers over the street.

The locale has been home to successive waves of immigrants – Huguenots, Jews and recently Bengalis. The Huguenots left their mark with the magnificent silk merchants' house on Fournier Street, which meets Brick Lane by the Jamme Masjid mosque. Of the Jewish presence little remains except Katz's shop at number 92 that sold only string – kosher string, mind.

Address Brick Lane, E1 | Getting there Underground to Aldgate East (District and Hammersmith & City lines); Overground to Shoreditch High Street; bus 8 or 388 | Hours Accessible 24 hours | Tip The street would not be complete without a bookshop – the Brick Lane Bookshop at no. 166 is just about the only one in the whole of the East End.

15 Bud Flanagan Plaque
Tribute to the quintessential voice of England

The voice of the endearing Spitalfields-born Chaim Reuben Weintrop (1896 – 1968), better known as Bud Flanagan, is still heard every week on TV singing the sublimely executed 1940s' pastiche 'Who Do You Think You Are Kidding, Mr Hitler?', the theme tune of the classic comedy *Dad's Army*.

That this most reassuringly English of voices existed at all was all down to local Jewish leaders insisting that the children of immigrants did not speak Yiddish and were Anglicised into the local culture. Weintrop came from a Polish-Jewish family who paid for a ticket from Hamburg to New York and like so many were conned into thinking they'd landed in the Big Apple when they were turfed out at the Irongate Stairs by the Tower of London. He was raised here above a fish and chip shop with six siblings and made his stage debut in 1908 in a talent contest at the London Music Hall performing conjuring tricks as 'Fargo, the Boy Wizard'.

In 1910, aged 14, Weintrop walked to Southampton to get a job on a ship as an electrician. He stayed on in New York where he sold newspapers, delivered telegrams and went west to harvest wheat in the prairies, travelling to Fargo, North Dakota, solely because it had the same name as his magic act. Weintrop returned to Britain to fight in the Great War and was sent to serve in France. As a soldier he took the name Robert Winthrop as it didn't sound Jewish. He was bullied by a sergeant major called Bud Flanagan. Weintrop was so humiliated by the officer he vowed revenge by turning the man's name into a laughing stock.

With Chesney Allen, Bud Flanagan formed the double act Flanagan and Allen who later became part of the anarchic Crazy Gang team. During the 1940s they recorded two of the era's most famous songs: 'We're Going To Hang Out the Washing on the Siegfried Line', which mocked the Germans' defences.

Address 12 Hanbury Street, Spitalfields E1 6QR | **Getting there** Overground to Shoreditch High Street | **Hours** Accessible 24 hours | **Tip** Further east along Hanbury Street, at the back of the old brewery, is the spot where the Ripper's second victim, Annie Chapman, was discovered in 1888.

16__Cable Street Mural

London's famous anti-fascist mural

A magnificent coloured depiction of the Battle of Cable Street, one of the defining events in East End history, can be found on the wall of St George's Town Hall, halfway along lengthy Cable Street.

The Battle of Cable Street took place on Sunday 4 October, 1936. It was mostly a stand-off between the paramilitary British Union of Fascists, the Blackshirts, led by former Tory MP and Labour Cabinet Minister Oswald Mosley, and an opposition of locals, Jews and communists. The Blackshirts wanted to antagonise the East End's Jewish population and amassed a huge army of supporters, so the police sent some 6,000 officers – a third of the Met's force –into the area that morning.

On Cable Street they found the barricade of an overturned lorry alongside barrels, corrugated iron, timber, paving stones and piles of bricks, all set in place to stop the Blackshirts marching through. Crowds surged through the area down Leman Street from noon, the police keeping opponents at bay. At 3.30pm, the fascist leader Mosley's open-top Bentley, surrounded by bodyguards, crept towards the junction of Dock Street and Cable Street, flanked by police motorcycle outriders. An autogiro (an early type of helicopter) flew overhead. Opponents showered a volley of stones and bricks at the motorcade. One smashed the window of Mosley's car. Another struck him in the face. Mosley gave a Hitler-style salute as his car was attacked by a band of Jewish heavies. The home secretary, John Simon, then called off the march. Fascism lost the day. Eighty-four people were arrested and taken to Leman Street police station, where the floor and walls became covered with the blood of those who had been beaten by the police.

The mural was painted between 1979 and 1983 by a team that included Dave Binnington, Paul Butler, Ray Walker and Desmond Rochfort. The original design was by Dave Binnington.

Address St George's Town Hall, Cable Street, Shadwell E1 0DR | Getting there Overground to Shadwell; bus 100 or D3 | Hours Accessible 24 hours | Tip Head north to Leman Street police station where those arrested at the Battle were taken, the Jews among them more severely beaten up.

17 Canary Wharf

The ultimate in conspicuous millennial consumerism

It is not an idle boast to describe Canary Wharf as the most ambitious regeneration project of early 21st-century Europe. Here the land around the three West India Docks, at the northern end of the Isle of Dogs, has been transformed into a new city in gleaming glass and granite, bold and brilliant, towers reaching to the sky filled with gilt-edge companies, expensive shops and flats, alongside high-quality transport links.

Canary Wharf gained its name from the boxes of bananas from the Canary Islands unloaded here in the days when these were busy docks. When they closed in 1980, the Thatcher government created the London Docklands Development Corporation to stimulate redevelopment. Construction began in 1988 with Olympia & York, major property developers, in charge. A huge boost was the new Docklands Light Railway. By 1991, no. 1 Canada Square, so-named because Olympia & York was a Toronto company, and still popularly known as Canary Wharf itself, had been built, its lofty elevation reminding those who could see it across London of the arrival of the new Canary Wharf. For long it was the tallest building in Britain. Ironically by the time it opened, the London commercial property market had collapsed. A new company was formed and the project saved.

The 1999 opening of the Jubilee line as a fast underground line linking the regenerated waterside areas with central London completed the picture. Canary Wharf tube station, designed by Norman Foster, is so large that no. 1 Canada Square tower could fit inside it. Not everyone was impressed. The City of London was initially aghast, but then realised increased competition would benefit both areas. Prince Charles noted: 'Personally, I would go mad if I had to work in a place like that!' Nevertheless, scores of major companies migrated east, resulting in a workforce that now numbers more than a hundred thousand.

Address 1 Canada Square, E14 5AB | Getting there Underground (Jubilee line) or DLR to Canary Wharf | Hours Accessible 24 hours | Tip 1 Canada Square, often erroneously called Canary Wharf, is simply the most famous of a large collection of clever and brilliant towers in the vicinity. It is no longer the highest. That honour went in 2019 to Landmark Pinnacle by Squire and Partners.

18 The Carpenters' Arms

The Kray pub – setting for a dreadful murder

Visitors drawn to the East End's unfortunate history come to this popular pub, just off Brick Lane, not just for the excellent ambience and alcohol but to search the outside wall for signs of one of the most farcical shootings in the history of local of gangland warfare.

In January 1965, Ginger Marks, a local villain, was shot dead outside the pub by Freddie Foreman, the south London enforcer. But it was by mistake. Foreman had been driving around Bethnal Green looking for Marks' associate, Jimmy Evans. Eventually Foreman spotted Marks and Evans walking along Cheshire Street eating chips. He drove up, leaned out of the window, and aimed his .38 revolver at the pair.

Evans, with brilliant recourse to his own safety, grabbed Marks, using him as a human shield to protect himself from Foreman's bullets. Marks died instantly. The police concluded he had probably been shot in the stomach, as they found a chip embedded in the wall of the pub, the hole apparently still there. Marks' body was never found. Rumours spread that a compliant undertaker had inserted his corpse into an already filled coffin as in one of Arthur Conan Doyle's Sherlock Holmes short stories. Foreman was acquitted of the murder and told journalists that his only regret was that he 'didn't shoot the two of them that night.'

In those days the pub was owned by the Kray twins. Their boxing gloves were hanging on the wall behind the bar and the counter was made from coffin lids. Every weekend their infamous, omnipotent mother, Violet, would hold court here surrounded by her overdressed, bejewelled friends sporting huge peroxide beehive hairdos.

The survival of the pub is remarkable. So many similar nearby traditional Ben Truman houses have since called last orders, including the Crown and Anchor a few hundred yards from the Cheshire Arms where the Krays hired Judy Garland to sing one Saturday night in 1965.

Address 73 Cheshire Street, Bethnal Green E2 6EG | Getting there Overground to Shoreditch High Street | Hours Daily 3pm – midnight | Tip The Krays' house at nearby 178 Vallance Road, from where they operated their powerful 1960s' crime empire, has been replaced by a newer property. There is a plaque on the wall, but it is for Prince Charles opening the new estate, not the gangland bosses.

19_ Cereal Killer Café

Breakfast any time in corn flake heaven

Accusations of tastelessness deep in the heart of Ripper territory aside, this is a unique and original venture. A café serving nothing other than, yes you guessed it, cereals, 120 of them – from All Bran to Weetos and everything in between.

The venture opened in 2014 and is the brainchild of Belfast-born identical twins Alan and Gary Keery who while hungover in Shoreditch one morning fancied a 'nice cold bowl of cereal for lunch.' They Googled 'cereal café London', discovered nothing like that existed, and went home to bran the plan. Naturally they chose the East End as their location. 'It is a place where creative ideas work.'

Detractors were quick to sneer. A business course mentor swore that nobody would eat cereal after 10 o'clock, 'you'll have to serve sandwiches.' Channel 4 accused them of being out-of-touch 'hipsters' for selling marked-up cereal in a borough with high rates of poverty. But once they opened, the story went viral. Customers poured in. A sheikh from Dubai Snapchatted and within a year or two the Keerys had opened a branch in Dubai. Qatar came next. There are also branches in Camden and Birmingham.

It wasn't the strange looks from people walking past that became a problem but the manic protestors. The anarchist group Class War stormed the café in protest, daubed red paint on the shop front and graffitied the word 'scum' on the windows. The Keerys thought it was a joke at first until the manager told them there was a mob outside with pitchforks and pig masks. The protesters' beef was that 'communities are being ripped apart – by Russian oligarchs, Saudi sheikhs, Israeli scumbag property developers, Texan oil-money tw*ts and our own homegrown Eton toffs … We don't want pop-up gin bars, we want community.'

It didn't put them off. Boris Johnson soon came along to show solidarity. He had a bowl of the chocolate malt cereal, Milo.

Address 192a Brick Lane, Spitalfields E1 6SA, +44 (0)203 601 9100, www.cerealkillercafe.co.uk | Getting there Overground to Shoreditch High Street | Hours Daily 9am–7pm | Tip Visitors to Brick Lane are spoiled for choice when it comes to food. The best beigel shop in London is at nearby no. 159 while most of this very long street is lined with curry restaurants.

20 __ Charles Dickens' Six Jolly Fellowship Porters

The Grapes pub, immortalised by Dickens

One of only half a dozen surviving riverside East End pubs and dating back to around 1720, the Grapes has a unique place in local literary history. It was captured by Charles Dickens as the Six Jolly Fellowship Porters in his greatest and last full novel, *Our Mutual Friend* (1865), in which the Thames flows throughout this satire of the rich:

'The bar of the Six Jolly Fellowship Porters was a bar to soften the human breast … This haven was divided from the rough world by a glass partition and a half-door, with a leaden sill upon it for the convenience of resting your liquor; but, over this half-door the bar's snugness so gushed forth that, albeit customers drank there standing, in a dark and draughty passage where they were shouldered by other customers passing in and out …'

In 2011 the pub was bought by the great Shakespearean actor Ian McKellen who is often seen at the Monday night pub quiz. 'I came here because of the river. You are in the middle of the city but all you can see is water and sky.' Earlier owners tried to insist the landlady install a fruit machine. A sign placed on it read: *This must never be used*. Two weeks later it was removed. The pub welcomes dogs, but explains that it does not have a licence to admit children.

The site was perfectly chosen. Next door, no. 78, is the long-time home of the 1970s' foreign secretary David Owen (see ch. 69). At no. 80 Britain's greatest 20th-century painter, Francis Bacon, lived in the 1960s. His lover, George Dyer, planted cannabis inside and one day Bacon was arrested. Other neighbours have included the legendary mid-20th-century film director David Lean (*Great Expectations*, fittingly) who installed a huge turntable on the ground floor of his home that would fit his Rolls-Royce.

Address 76 Narrow Street, Limehouse E14 8BP, +44 (0)207 987 4396, www.thegrapes.co.uk | **Getting there** Limehouse DLR and National Rail | **Hours** Mon–Sat noon–11pm, Sun noon–10.30pm | **Tip** *Flâneurs* looking for other local literary links could head east to Limehouse Causeway, the extension to Narrow Street, where George Orwell dossed, as recounted in his 1933 work *Down and Out in Paris and London*.

21 Christ Church Spitalfields

The East End's most majestic church

Christ Church, which opened in 1729, was designed by the greatest of East End architects, Nicholas Hawksmoor, a pupil of Christopher Wren. It was built as part of the Tories' Fifty New Churches Act of 1711, devised to 'Christianise people in or near the cities of London or Westminster,' in an area rife with non-conformity. The Act stipulated that such churches were made of 'Stone and other proper Materials' and its spire soars high above the nearby weavers' houses.

Christ Church's positioning was not random. Hawksmoor set his London churches according to biblical measurements – 'sacred geometry' – measurements mentioned in the Bible as to how key buildings in cities should be arranged. The main measurement Hawksmoor, and indeed Wren in reshaping London after the Fire of 1666, used was the Hebrews' 2,000 cubits, a cubit being the length from the elbow to the tip of the fingers, differing from person to person, but in this case the cubit of the architect, and totalling some two-thirds of a mile. In this way Hawksmoor set Christ Church Spitalfields 2,000 cubits from his Danish church in Marine (now Wellclose) Square and 2,000 cubits from St Mary Woolnoth by the modern-day Bank tube station.

The churchyard was known in the early 20th century as Itchy Park on account of the lice-infected vagrants who dossed there. In 1978, a group of enthusiasts launched a campaign to restore the church. Heritage Lottery Fund money of £2.9 million was awarded in 1996 to repair the tower and spire. By 2000 the floor of the aisle galleries had been reinstated to Hawksmoor's original designs.

The church is the focus of Peter Ackroyd's 1985 mystery murder novel *Hawksmoor*, which interweaves the life of a modern-day detective, Nicholas Hawksmoor, with that of an 18th-century architect, Nicholas Dyer (based on Hawksmoor).

Address Commercial Street at Fournier Street, Spitalfields E1 6LY | Getting there Underground (Central, Circle and Hammersmith & City lines) and National Rail to Liverpool Street | Hours Intermittent during the week, plus Sunday morning | Tip At the other end of Fournier Street, in the beautiful Georgian enclave that leads from the church, can be found an 18th-century Wesleyan chapel that is now the Jamme Masjid Mosque.

22__Close-Up

Surprise cinema with impressive rentable library

If you manage not to miss the mysterious black, understated frontage you might think at first that you've wandered into a rather dignified and laid-back bookshop with obligatory even more laid-back café. Then you realise it's something really surprising and heart-warming: a secret cinema, a cinema club indeed, on shabby but chic Sclater Street in the epicentre of cool Shoreditch.

Close-Up has a state-of-the-art 40-seat cinema, one of the few cinemas in London that can show 35mm archival prints as well as 16mm prints, as with most films. But it is more than just an arthouse cinema club. In the age of Netflix, it also operates as London's last movie rental business. Damien Sanville, director and founder, moved to London in the late 1990s, having studied Philosophy and Fine Arts in Paris. He started Close-Up as a modest video library in 2005 at a nearby location. He launched a weekly film club in a number of venues, showing everything from early to contemporary cinema.

Then came the move to Sclater Street just at the right time, when the new Overground made it speedily accessible from much of London. Gradually ambition grew. Sanville has amassed over 20,000 rare books and DVDs, all covering film, after a bout of obsessive collecting. 'We wanted to bring in people who weren't necessarily aware of gems we had in our collection, and that proved successful … with films that are relevant to the history of the genre.' He also bought up *Vertigo* film magazine to put it online.

Sanville has jested that Close-Up is not tapping into the South Bank/NFT audience. 'The people that go to the NFT don't really come here as we don't appeal. Shoreditch is fashion, apps, graffiti and drunken people at the weekend. A large portion of London think of it as a shithole. If I didn't live here for all those years before, I wouldn't have found it "cool".'

Address 97 Sclater Street, Shoreditch E1 6HR, +44 (0)203 784 7970,
www.closeupfilmcentre.com | Getting there Overground to Shoreditch High Street | Hours
Daily noon–11.30pm | Tip One of the best known local locations used in a major film is
76 Quilter Street, half a mile to the north-east, home to the anxiety-ridden Cynthia in
Mike Leigh's 1997 drama *Secrets and Lies*.

23 Coldharbour

Home to Lord Nelson, Walter Raleigh and smugglers

This obscurely-sited L-shaped street is a remarkable find in a part of the Isle of Dogs that has been considerably redeveloped. Coldharbour, the name possibly a corruption of Coal Harbour, runs right by the Thames and is the only surviving remnant of the ancient hamlet of Blackwall, which was cut off from the rest of the Isle of Dogs by the building of the City Canal in 1805 that made the Isle an actual island.

Coldharbour was once described by John Betjeman, the much-loved late 20th-century poet laureate, as a place 'where some fine Georgian merchants' houses have the water washing up to their walls.' The first buildings here were put up by merchants working for the East India Company, whose ships left for the Far East from sites nearby after 1613. One of those is Isle House, one of the grandest and most glorious properties in the capital, built in 1824 for the Blackwall Dockmaster. Alongside, at no. 3, is the property where Admiral Nelson might have stayed in 1798 before leaving to fight in the Battle of Aboukir. Unfortunately, the house where the Elizabethan explorer and spy Walter Raleigh lodged has been demolished.

If it were just the houses, Coldharbour would be worth a visit, if only to see how the rich built themselves grand houses by the water. But to complete the picture is The Gun, a pub at the southern end, previously the King and Queen, Rose and Crown, and Ramsgate Pink (1750).

The Gun was built in 1716 and named in honour of the *Henry Addington* ship, which fired its guns from the river outside. Inside is a smart eating area and one of the best beer 'gardens' imaginable, set right by the water, which one can touch while gazing across the expanse for a magnificent view of the Millennium Dome. According to legend, Nelson and Emma Hamilton fraternised here and an underground passage connects the pub with no. 3 and its Nelson associations.

Address East off Preston's Road on the east side of the Isle of Dogs, E14 9NL | Getting there Blackwall DLR | Hours Accessible 24 hours | Tip There are no other streets of similar quality houses in the vicinity, the main attractions all being watery ones: the River Thames on the east, Blackwall Basin to the north-west and the huge stretch of the south section of the West India Dock to the south-west.

24 Columbia Market Gateposts

The sad last reminder of an epic Gothic edifice

All that is left of the vast Gothic Gormenghast that was the Victorian indoor Columbia Market are these two exquisitely fashioned gateposts at the western end of a street that is now home to London's leading weekend flower market.

Columbia Market was a gift to the costermongers and street traders from the vastly wealthy banking heiress Angela Burdett-Coutts. She inherited the Coutts bank fortune of nearly two million pounds to become England's richest woman in 1837, the year the throne was taken by Queen Victoria who, incidentally, was a visitor to Burdett-Coutts' parties at Holly Lodge, Highgate.

Burdett-Coutts bankrolled cotton gins in Nigeria, lifeboats in Brittany, and drinking fountains for dogs – even the statue of Greyfriars Bobby in Edinburgh. Charles Dickens directed her to East End poverty. Here she financed ragged schools and built model dwellings with £9000 of her own money. But her most glorious venture was Columbia Market, designed by Henry Darbishire and ready by 1864. It was a riot of soaring turrets, Tudor arches, cloisters and crypts, as glorious as St Pancras station's hotel or Manchester Town Hall.

Columbia Market meant that the traders could operate indoors regardless of the weather, rather than on the mean streets, but it was a flop. The costermongers preferred the open air. They despaired of rules outlawing Sunday opening on religious grounds, and mocked signs displayed on the walls urging them to *Be Sober, Be Vigilant, Be Pitiful, Be Courteous*. One poster that warned them not to swear or spit merely led to more swearing as they expectorated on the floor.

Columbia Market closed down in 1886. The grand Gothic castle was needlessly demolished in 1958. Columbia Road soon began to specialise in plants and flowers.

Address Columbia Road, Bethnal Green E2 7RG | Getting there Overground to Hoxton | Hours Accessible 24 hours | Tip Further east from the site of the demolished Columbia Market is the extraordinarily popular Columbia Road flower market, packed from pot to pot on a Sunday from 8am – 3pm.

25 Columbia Road Flower Market

London's greatest flower market

The East End has long specialised in the greatest markets, from the cheap and cheerful Whitechapel Waste to Petticoat Lane; from the sadly departed Club Row animal emporia to the vintage clothes shops off Brick Lane, and Sundays would not be complete without a visit to Columbia Road in the heart of Bethnal Green to savour the fabulously freakishly floral flower market, the best and busiest of its kind you will ever experience.

Columbia Road as a flower market came about by chance. What had been a depressing and disease-ridden slum in the 19th century was given an unlikely boost when the banking heiress Angela Burdett-Coutts built the Gothic monstrosity of Columbia Market on the street, enabling the costermongers to work indoors. It eventually failed as a venture and the building saw various changes of use before it was demolished after World War II. In its wake came a Saturday trading market more up-market than raucous Petticoat Lane. It was then moved to Sunday by Act of Parliament to aid the Jewish traders who wouldn't work on their Sabbath. Gradually more and more flower sellers began to appear in the 1970s, encouraged by the many gardening programmes on radio and TV.

The market opens up at 8am every Sunday. The traders, many of whom are second- or third-generation flower sellers, will have been there from 4am to set up their stalls to sell a wide range of houseplants, herbs, bulbs, shrubs, fresh-cut flowers, bedding plants and even 10-foot banana trees. The best bargains are to be found at just the right moment around 3pm as traders reduce their prices to shift the remaining stock.

It's not all about flowers. The market also has excellent shops in the permanent buildings, all of them independent ventures, selling cheese, antiques, soap and even Buddhist artefacts.

Address Columbia Road, Bethnal Green E2 7RG | Getting there Overground to Hoxton | Hours Flower market Sun 8am–3pm, although the road is accessible 24 hours | Tip Close by at 1a Goldsmith's Row is Hackney City Farm, which encourages children to learn about farmyard animals, the natural environment and growing vegetables.

26__ Concrete Overcoat for Mr Mitchell

Bizarre final resting place for Krays' irritant

Plans are occasionally announced to demolish the flyover that links Bow Road with High Street over the River Lea. If that ever does happen, East End criminologists might well be first on the scene to discover if the wrecking ball firms find any traces of human bones in the concrete supports. For according to one of the most colourful East End legends, somewhere inside the stone are the remains of Frank 'The Mad Axeman' Mitchell.

Mitchell, a huge psychopathic simpleton, was being held in Dartmoor Prison, locked up for holding a couple hostage with an axe, until a few weeks before Christmas 1966. While repairing fencing with fellow prisoners he walked off to feed some Dartmoor ponies, and somehow ended up in the back of the Krays' getaway car. Mitchell's escape made the front pages of the papers and launched the biggest manhunt ever seen in Britain. In London, the Krays holed him up in a house at 206a Barking Road, East Ham. Mitchell wasn't too pleased at being treated like a caged animal, not when the Krays had promised him he would be taken round the West End's leading nightspots, fêted as an underworld hero. Mitchell went down with a severe bout of cabin fever and threatened to shoot the Krays if he wasn't allowed out. On Christmas Eve the Kray twins' associates bundled Mitchell into a van and shot him dead on Barking Road.

But what happened to Mitchell's body? The agreed legend is that his corpse was embedded in the wet concrete propping up the then newly built Bow Flyover. During Ronnie Kray's funeral procession in 1995, 26 hearses crossed the river on this stretch of highway heading for Chingford Cemetery where Kray was to be buried. Given that the procession had no need to take this route, its inclusion was a bit suspicious.

Address Bow Flyover, E3 3BA | Getting there Overground to Bow Church DLR | Hours Accessible 24 hours | Tip The Krays' other Bow locations have been demolished but further west, along the main Mile End Road, is no. 106a, which in the 1960s was their Kentucky Club where guests included Barbara Windsor and Roger Moore.

27 __ Curry Mile
The street where curry rules

Perhaps the main thing that Brick Lane is known for, apart from the world's greatest beigel shop, and ultra-hip ventures such as Alcotraz and the Cereal Killer Café, are curry houses. This is, in fact, the longest such stretch in the UK. Curry's rise to the status of most popular English dish makes perfect sense; England taught India how to play cricket, so India taught the English how to appreciate a hot curry. It was ideal for a nation with an otherwise bland diet, as mercilessly sent up on the TV show *Goodness Gracious Me*. There are now more Indian restaurants in Greater London than in Delhi and Mumbai combined.

Surprisingly, it was as early as 1733 that curry was first served in London (on Haymarket). Curry had still not seeped into the national consciousness by the Victorian era, despite the Queen being Empress of India. In Thackeray's *Vanity Fair* novel, Mr Sedley insists that Becky Sharp tries some curry. When the heroine suffers 'torture' with the cayenne pepper, another character suggests she 'try a chilli.' ' "A chilli. Oh yes!" She thought a chilli was something cool, as its name suggested. "How fresh and green they look," she said, and put one into her mouth. It was hotter than the curry. "Water, for Heaven's sake, water!" she cried.'

After Indian independence and partition in 1947, many Asian seamen decided to stay in the capital and buy up bombed-out chippies and cafés to sell curry and rice alongside fish and chips. As curry became more popular, the British dishes were dropped. Bangladeshis now own some 65 per cent of all the supposed Indian restaurants. How ironic it should be in this legendary street, so imbued with anti-Asian racism in the 1970s, that curry is king. The only downside is the waiters' annoying habit of perching outside their establishment trying to drag the unwary into theirs – just theirs, as if it were the only one.

Address Brick Lane, Spitalfields E1 | Getting there Underground to Aldgate East (District and Hammersmith & City lines); Overground to Shoreditch High Street; bus 8 or 388 | Hours Varies with each restaurant's opening hours | Tip In recent decades, the more discerning diner has headed for the curry houses around New Road, Whitechapel, such as Tayyab's (see ch. 91).

28 Dennis Severs' House

Remarkable Huguenot 'experience' in a period house

The late Californian artist Dennis Severs turned his exquisite Georgian home, bought in 1979, into a Huguenot 'experience' that takes visitors back in a time capsule to the 18th century, the time when the devout austere French Protestant sect brought silk weaving to London.

Severs, who once recalled that at school he was regarded as somewhere between 'exceptional' and 'mentally retarded', wanted visitors to feel that they had passed through the surface of a painting into an 'historical imagination. I worked inside out to create what turned out to be a collection of atmospheres: moods that harbour the light and the spirit of various ages,' he once explained. Rather than simply restore the house, Severs wanted to 'bring it to life as my home. With a candle, a chamber pot and a bedroll, I began sleeping in each of the house's 10 rooms so that I might arouse my intuition in the quest for each room's soul.'

As people make their way through the property, they are taken on a journey through the 18th and 19th centuries with the fictional Jervis family. Each room is designed in a different period style, even with different smells. Rooms have been laid out as if they are still in use, with bits of half-eaten bread, and as if the Jervis family have only just left. The historian Raphael Samuel considered it 'a magical mystery tour which dazzles the visitor with a succession of scenes more crowded with memorable incident than the mere facsimile of what passes in the museums as a period room.' The motto of the house is *Aut Visum Aut Non!*: 'You either see it or you don't'.

When Severs moved here in 1979, Spitalfields was dilapidated and derelict, although the even more *outré* artists, Gilbert and George, lived nearby on Fournier Street. He was drawn to what he called 'English light'. Since then, the area has undergone a spectacular revival with Dennis Severs House as the strangest attraction.

Address 18 Folgate Street, Spitalfields E1 6BX, +44 (0)207 247 4013,
www.dennissevershouse.co.uk | Getting there Underground to Liverpool Street (Central,
Circle and Hammersmith & City lines) | Hours Sun noon–4pm, Mon noon–2pm, 5–9pm,
Wed & Fri 5–9pm; private tours by appointment | Tip Remarkably, Folgate Street is just
one of half a dozen exquisite Georgian streets that survive in this small enclave between
Norton Folgate and Brick Lane.

29 — Drape Seated Woman
Henry Moore sculpture returns to the East End

On a street overseen by the lofty towers of Canary Wharf, now one of the most vibrant working areas of London, rests a bronze sculpture created in 1958 by the great modernist Henry Moore. It was moved here in 2015, after years on loan to the Yorkshire Sculpture Park, but from 1962 to 1977 it had lived in the East End in the since demolished Stifford Estate in Stepney where residents had nicknamed her 'Old Flo'.

This cast was originally acquired by the now defunct London County Council as part of their Patronage of the Arts Scheme (1957–65) which, in a rare example of progressive municipal policy, allocated 0.1 per cent of its building budget for the purchase of artworks. The intention was that public art could help create a sense of community and identity in new estates; that art could enrich people's lives in the poorest places; that nothing was too good for them – and children could clamber over her as it wasn't surrounded by a fence. Henry Moore sold the council the sculpture at a minimal price. The Stifford Estate also featured murals by artist Anthony Holloway, the ingenious creator of the experimental stained-glass windows in Manchester Cathedral, but these were lost when the tower blocks were demolished.

With Old Flo moving to Yorkshire, Tower Hamlets council seemed to have forgotten they were owners of a major work of art worth some £5 million. That was until the mayor of Tower Hamlets and Conservative councillor Tim Archer heard about Old Flo and started a campaign to bring her back. There was opposition. Some detractors said the council should sell the work and spend the proceeds on affordable housing. The council launched a competition to find a suitable home, and Canary Wharf was successful. Ironically this meant that far from having the artefact in a working-class area, it was now in one of the most exclusive enclaves in the world!

Address Cabot Square, Canary Wharf E14 4QA | Getting there Underground (Jubilee line) and DLR to Canary Wharf | Hours Accessible 24 hours | Tip The Canary Wharf estate, an almost entirely 21st-century project, has one of the largest collections of public art in London. For instance, Jay Battle's *Vanishing Point* at Westferry Circus looks like the shell of a sea creature while Emma Biggs' *Pattern for Democracy* rests on the floor of the exclusive Canary Wharf shopping centre.

30 Driverless DLR trains

Britain's most advanced public transport

Britain's most hi-tech trains take tens of thousands of workers, residents and tourists every day through the very core of the East End, in particular the old docks, on the Docklands Light Railway (DLR) where the lack of a visible presence steering the train foxes hordes of schoolchildren intent on knocking at the window to annoy the driver.

The railway opened in 1987 when it had only 15 stations and 2 routes, Island Gardens to Tower Gateway or Stratford, and so detractors were quick to denounce the DLR as a 'toy town line to nowhere.' However, the phenomenal growth of Canary Wharf, where 100,000 now work, saw the line expand and eventually cross the Thames into south London. It keeps on growing.

Ironically, much of the network uses the viaducts built for the earliest railway in the area, the Fenchurch Street to Blackwall Railway of 1840. That railway was so low-tech, trains were pulled up the slope by cable. The poet John Betjeman noted in 1952 how 'like stagecoaches they rumbled past East End chimney pots, wharves and shipping stopping at empty black stations till they came to a final halt at Blackwall station.' What a contrast with the modern-day, booming DLR!

Much politics went into the DLR's gestation. The Thatcher government ensured it was designed and built entirely by the private sector, and that Ken Livingstone's left-wing Greater London Council could not get their hands on it. Powering the DLR with overhead cables was ruled out by the government as they didn't want the vehicles to look like trams. One minister told workers: 'Trams come from socialist countries. We are not a socialist country!' Driverless trains meant no drivers' strikes.

Strangely, the only accidents have occurred when the trains have been guided manually, such as when one vehicle toppled and hung over the edge at the original Island Gardens terminus in 1987.

Address From Stratford in the north to Lewisham in the south, Woolwich Arsenal in the east and Bank in the west | Hours Mon–Sat 5.30–12.30am, Sun 7am–11.30pm | Tip An equally picturesque alternative to the trains is to traverse the East End by water. Services on the Thames boats stop at the Tower, Canary Wharf and Masthouse Terrace on the Isle of Dogs.

31 East India Dock Basin
All that's left of Britain's most powerful docks

The East India Dock Basin was where, in the 18th and 19th centuries, ships delivered their prized and valuable cargoes from the Far East. It is now a wildlife sanctuary featuring kingfishers, black redstarts and common terns.

East India Docks were built between 1803 and 1806 to handle Asian trade: spices, indigo, silk, Persian carpets and tea, the latter a business worth around £30 million a year. Of the tea clipper ships, protected here by a well-trained, well-paid paramilitary workforce, the most famous was the *Cutty Sark* that now stands in dry dock on the opposite bank at Greenwich.

In contrast to the other docks, at East India there were no dockside warehouses. The produce that arrived was too valuable to be kept that way and so was taken under armed guard along a new road, Commercial Road, now a major highway, to the company's warehouses off Petticoat Lane. The opening of the East India Docks saw crime fall. In the three years before the docks opened, more than 200 chests of tea were stolen. In the next three years none went missing; thieves had to make do with stuffing handfuls of loose tea into their pockets instead.

Steam power and larger ships reduced the importance of the East India Docks, and during the 20th century most of the trade dwindled away. However, one unexpected use for the docks came during World War II when the Allies' floating Mulberry harbours used in the D-Day landings were made here. In 1967, the East India Docks were the first to close when the new container ships that could be unloaded near motorways in the suburbs changed the need to journey into the capital. In the 1980s most of these docks were filled in, and the high walls that protected them were knocked down, in what was a short-sighted decision by the authorities who then realised the potential of the sites and began renovating the old docks instead of removing them.

Address Between the Lower Lea Crossing and the River Thames | **Getting there** Overground to East India DLR | **Hours** Accessible 24 hours | **Tip** It's not easy trying to find traces of what were three huge stretches of water forming the East India Docks. Of the Export Dock, next to nothing remains. Of the Import Dock about one-third remains between Saffron Avenue and the fast A1261.

32 East London Mosque

The largest mosque in Britain

The East London Mosque, able to accommodate some 7,000 worshippers, towers over Whitechapel. It serves Britain's largest Muslim community, which is based in Whitechapel and Spitalfields, mostly consisting of Bangladeshis.

As London had no mosque at the beginning of the 20th century, despite the Empire housing tens of millions of Muslims, a meeting was held at the Ritz Hotel on 9 November, 1910 to establish a fund for organising weekly Friday prayers and create a permanent place of worship in London. The original trustees even included the first Lord Rothschild. In 1940, three houses were bought at 446–448 Commercial Road, Ratcliffe, the site chosen because it was near the various London Docks, used by thousands of South Asian seamen.

During the 1950s the number of immigrants from Sylhet in what was then East Pakistan and is now Bangladesh rose from 2,000 in 1951 to 6,000 in 1961. The numbers continued to increase, especially in the East End, so a major mosque was needed. Instead of building it at Ratcliffe, the founders chose a site closer to the centre of the East End's Bangladeshi community. The Greater London Council made a compulsory purchase order on the land, which was a bomb site. Construction began in 1982 to the designs of John Gill Associates. The mosque is topped with a golden dome and there are several powerful minarets.

The mosque became one of the first in the UK to use loudspeakers to broadcast the *adhan* call to prayer over the community. Some locals protested, citing 'noise pollution', a story carried in the tabloids, but challenged by local Church of England clerics. As the clergy are keen to impress, 'We have a history of working with people of other faiths and with people of no faith.' Significantly, for many years the site incorporated a tiny synagogue that the mosque elders fought unsuccessfully to save.

Address 82–92 Whitechapel Road, Whitechapel E1 1JQ | Getting there Underground (District and Hammersmith & City lines) and Overground to Whitechapel | Hours Daily 10am–11pm | Tip A few hundred yards to the west on Adler Street is Altab Ali Park, named after a young Bangladeshi chased along Brick Lane and murdered there in 1978. The open land there marks the site of the original white chapel that gave the area its name.

33 Execution Dock

Grim reminder of the traditional fate pirates met

Execution Dock in Wapping was where pirates were hanged from gibbets, visible to everyone on the river, *pour encourager les autres*, being kept there until three tides had washed over them. The site is now overlooked by a pub named after one of the most infamous to meet his fate this way, Captain Kidd, hanged on 23 May, 1701.

Those captured and brought to London were first taken to Marshalsea Prison in Southwark, and from there led on a cart to Execution Dock by the Admiralty Marshal who was seated on a horse and carrying a silver oar. Particularly awful felons would first be covered with tar, their head fixed in a metal harness as the flesh rotted away. When the victim had finished making his last speech, the cart on which he was standing would be driven away, leaving him hanging.

In the 18th century, convict ships were moored on the Thames near the marshes at the edge of the East End. On board were felons bound for Australia who lived in miserable conditions. They were up at 5am for breakfast of 12 ounces of bread and a pint of cocoa. Hard labour finished around 6pm after which they would be rowed back for meals of 'ox cheek, pease and mould-covered biscuits.'

Captain (William) Kidd was a Scottish mercenary who killed one of his own crewmen in 1697. While awaiting trial confined in London's Newgate Prison, he begged William IV for clemency. He was taken for execution nonetheless. However, when the men holding the line attached to Kidd's neck rode away the rope snapped. Kidd fell to the ground still alive. He was lifted up again; this time the rope stayed, and he was hanged. His body was left to hang by the Thames at Tilbury, further east, not here, for three years. Many believed he left hidden treasure including 200 bars of gold. A wreck was found off Madagascar and a search yielded a supposedly silver bar, which turned out to be 95 per cent lead.

Address River Thames, behind the Captain Kidd pub, 108 Wapping High Street, Wapping E1W 2NE | Getting there Overground to Wapping; bus 100 | Hours Accessible 24 hours | Tip Few Wapping riverside pubs remain, but those that do are some of the most popular in the East End and enjoy the most colourful of names, including the Town of Ramsgate (62 Wapping High Street) and the Prospect of Whitby (57 Wapping Wall).

34 Explorers' Leaving Point

Watery launch pad to open up the world

The stairs leading down to the Thames by the Prospect of Whitby pub in Wapping act as a reminder of the first steps countless explorers took when leaving the East End to map the world.

The first of these expeditions took place in 1553 when Sir Hugh Willoughby went in search of the North-East Passage to China, avoiding Constantinople by heading north of Scandinavia and Russia into the Arctic wastes. The aim was to participate in the lucrative spice trade then closed off to the West. Willoughby had no nautical experience and was chosen for his leadership skills. His party left in three ships on 10 May. At the Scandinavian North Cape, they were overcome by a storm and the ships became separated. Willoughby was trapped in the Lapland ice, and he and his men froze to death. They were found by Russian fishermen a year later. His deputy, Richard Chancellor, fared better, journeying alone across the Russian White Sea to Moscow, where he met Ivan the Terrible. This led to the foundation of the Muscovy Company that hugely boosted trade between London and Russia.

William Borough, mentioned on a nearby memorial, was the late 16th-century Comptroller of the Navy who drew up some of the earliest maps of Russia. Also mentioned is Martin Frobisher. He left Ratcliffe Cross with 35 men in two ships on 7 June, 1576, calling at the Netherlands to drop off a group of convicts. He then headed west, spurred on by a home-made course in geometry from John Dee, the 'black magician' of Mortlake and Queen Elizabeth's personal astrologer. When his ship approached two large bodies of land in northern Canada, Frobisher explained to the crew that the northern mass was Asia and the southern America; it was two parts of Baffin Island. The party landed and clashed with the locals, one of whom they seized and brought back with them to the East End where he died from a cold soon after arriving.

Address Steps by the Prospect of Whitby pub, 57 Wapping Wall, Wapping E1W 3SH | Getting there Overground to Wapping | Hours Accessible 24 hours | Tip To the north, between Wapping Wall and Glamis Road, is a monstrous looking swing bridge that used to rise to let ships enter Shadwell Docks. The hydraulic power was provided by the nearby London Hydraulic Power Company. Tower Bridge, a mile west, still uses hydraulic power.

35 Fish Island

Quite a catch, the latest bohemian enclave

Fish Island isn't really an island and the fish are rather inconspicuous, but this once-forgotten enclave by the Hertford Union Canal sandwiched, or rather battered, between Victoria Park and Queen Elizabeth Park is one of the new 21st-century East End's go-to places.

What was a decrepit, ex-industrial forgotten land has been cleverly revived, the name taken simply from the street names: Bream, Dace and Roach. It has been revamped with new homes, businesses and an edge of creativity, major improvements in footways and roads linking it with the post-2012 Olympic Park.

Historically, Pye Road, the main Roman route linking London to Colchester, passed through the area and probably crossed the River Lea by what is now Fish Island. Industrialisation brought nasty stuff: crude oil, coal tar, ink and rubber works. By end of the 19th century, some 6,000 people were living here, working for firms such as the Gas Light and Coke Company. Things weren't helped during the 20th century by the installation of waste disposal facilities. Yet the best known local concern was Percy Dalton's Peanut Company on Dace Road. Nowadays, one of the most famous institutions on Fish Island is also in the food business: H. Forman and sons, legendary salmon smokers, who even boast of an EU-protected 'London Cure' for their recipe. Forman's was forcibly removed from nearby Stratford when the Olympics moved in but now has a restaurant and benefits from being only two minutes from West Ham United.

The most remarkable story though is the reappearance of Ben Truman, the East End's best-known brewery, long thought to be consigned to the slops of history but now brewing again from Fish Island. Fish Island is changing constantly. It remains to be seen whether it becomes another Stratford (soulless high-rises and naff chain stores) or a new Shoreditch (bohemian outlets and creativity).

Address Between Dace Road and the River Lea Navigation, E3 | Getting there Overground to Hackney Wick | Hours Accessible 24 hours | Tip The adjacent River Lea and its tributaries are a fisherman's delight. The waters are full of coarse fish: carp, bream, tench, pike, perch, barbel, chub, roach, rudd and large eels. Fittingly, it was the River Lea that was the setting for Isaac Walton's 17th-century *The Compleat Angler*.

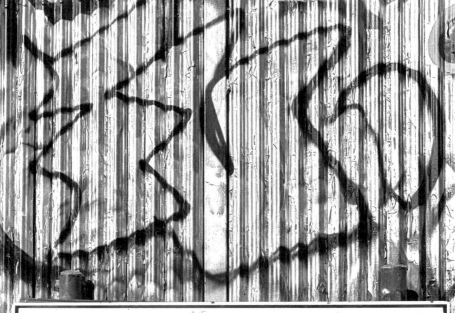

36 Four Per Cent Industrial Dwellings

Reminder of a key charitable housing project

The inscription on the arch here at the non-market western end of Wentworth Street reads: *Erected by the Four Per Cent Industrial Dwellings Company Ltd, 1886.* It was moved to this more prominent position from nearby Thrawl Street and is all that remains of the housing estate built here by the Rothschilds for poor Jews.

The previous year, Natty, the first Lord Rothschild, formed the Four Per Cent Industrial Dwellings Company with other leading Jews. They were spurred on by the mainstream United Synagogue whose inquiry into 'spiritual destitution' in the East End in 1884 found that physical hardships were more pressing. Rothschild had stated 'we now have a new Poland on our hands in East London. Our business is to humanise … and Anglicise them.'

The company agreed to limit profits to 4 per cent, rather than the usual 8 per cent other property companies aimed for. The capital outlay was £50,000 in 5,000 shares of £10 each. Within a decade, the company had built acceptable accommodation for hundreds. Each home had two rooms with a central corridor, a shared toilet and a kitchen. Some 150 families were housed here and 1,500 across the other five similar blocks in the East End. The estates were not restricted to Jews.

By the 1970s, the Four Per Cent Dwellings were in disrepair, and were demolished. Meanwhile, the once vast Jewish population in the East End was in decline, to be replaced by Bangladeshi immigrants, treated to an apartheid housing policy. Tower Hamlets kept properties empty, reserved for white occupants, which meant that about half of all homeless people in the borough were Bengali. In the 1980s, the council ruled that the children of families who had lived in the East End for over 20 years had priority. This was finally declared racist in the 1990s.

ERECTED BY THE
FOUR PER CENT INDUSTRIAL DWELLINGS COMPANY LTD

1886

Address Wentworth Street, Spitalfields E1 6LR | Getting there Underground to Aldgate East (District and Hammersmith & City lines) | Hours Accessible 24 hours | Tip An arch on nearby Brick Lane proclaims the existence of what is often now referred to as Banglatown and indicates how, as the Jewish population moved out in the late 20th century, Bangladeshis moved in.

37 Gandhi's London Residence

Passing home of the great Indian spiritual leader

There have been many world famous and surprising visitors to the East End: Joe Stalin, Lenin, Trotsky … and even the great Indian spiritual leader Mahatma Gandhi. The Mahatma came to London in 1931 for round-table talks on Indian independence. Typically, he rejected the chance of staying in the kind of luxurious hotel usually chosen for visiting overseas dignitaries, and decided to stay in a working-class community in Bromley-by-Bow. His residence was here, Kingsley Hall, a hostel run by volunteers, now a community centre, 'set among the rotting row houses, smelly gas works and soap factories,' according to his biographer, James D. Hunt.

Kingsley Hall had been established three years earlier by two sisters, Muriel and Doris Lester, inspired by their Christian beliefs, and named after their brother who died young. The sisters' mantra was 'Peace, Temperance and Women's Rights'. Muriel Lester had visited Gandhi's ashram in India in 1925. Like Gandhi, who was a member of the high Brahmin caste, she had rejected her middle-class upbringing and chosen to live a frugal life. Kingsley Hall was a 'teetotal public house'.

The sisters' decision to put up Gandhi did not meet with universal acclaim. Among many hostile letters was one that read: 'Repent! How can you entertain an old devil like Gandhi. What can you be thinking about – an Englishwoman … Black people should know their place.'

When Gandhi arrived, the Pathé newsreel pointed out how the 'bizarre little man' was still wearing his trademark loincloth as he got off his ship amid heavy rain at Folkestone. He stayed for 12 weeks. His visitors included a remarkable collection of celebrities including the actor Charlie Chaplin and the playwright George Bernard Shaw.

Address Kingsley Hall, 21 Powis Road, Bromley-by-Bow E3 3HJ | Getting there Underground to Bromley-by-Bow (District and Hammersmith & City lines); bus 488 | Hours Intermittent, but normal working hours; the hall is also open during Open House Weekend in September | Tip Venturing out into the heart of the East End in 1931, Gandhi would go for walks along the top of the Northern Outfall Sewer, now the Greenway, a major route for joggers and walkers.

38__George Orwell's Ministry of Love Inspiration

Former police station vexed Orwell

The grim cells of the Ministry of Love, 'the really frightening one' from George Orwell's dystopian work *1984*, are based on the cells of the former Bethnal Green police station.

It was here at Christmas 1931 that Orwell (real name Eric Blair) was incarcerated for a few hours after deliberately getting himself arrested for being drunk and disorderly – just to see what a jail was like. As part of the scam, he went to a rough pub, and downed whisky and beer on an empty stomach before stumbling out, unable to feel his legs. When Orwell saw two policemen coming towards him he took a whisky bottle from his pocket and began swigging before falling down. It worked. The coppers frog-marched him here and locked him up overnight. Orwell gave his name as Edward Burton, said he had been disowned by his parents, and was living on casual work at Billingsgate. Orwell perversely hoped to be mistreated, as that would make better copy, but instead he was treated well, fed with bread, marge and tea, and the sergeant's wife's meat and potatoes. He spent the night counting the porcelain bricks on the walls, just as Winston Smith does in the book.

Orwell often spent time in the East End looking for inspiration. He was overcome with middle-class guilt, having been to Eton and then serving in the British Imperial Police in Burma. He went 'suitably disguised to Limehouse and Whitechapel [to] sleep in common lodging-houses and pal up with dock labourers, street hawkers, derelict people, beggars, and, if possible, criminals.' On his first mission roughing it he walked an enormous distance from Notting Hill to Limehouse Causeway to lodge in a doss house in what was then seedy Chinatown, experiences retold in his first work, *Down and Out in Paris and London* (1933).

Address 458 Bethnal Green Road, Bethnal Green E2 0DJ | **Getting there** Underground to Bethnal Green (Central line); bus 8 or 388 | **Hours** Viewable from the outside only | **Tip** The fundamentalist proletarian yet upper middle-class Orwell would have approved of Pellicci's at 332 Bethnal Green Road, E2 0AG. It is now the sole remaining authentic traditional working-class café in the area, famed for its ornate, panelled wooden décor for which it has been awarded Grade II listed status by English Heritage.

39 Gilbert and George Land

The living embodiment of bohemian Spitalfields

Living ghosts, wonderfully eccentric, ever playful *outré* artists, Gilbert and George are the very essence of 'out there' unconventionality, dressed in the most absurdly normal conventional clothes. They live very conspicuously on Fournier Street, the exquisite Georgian street full of Huguenot merchants' houses, their two addresses – home and workshop – part of their *oeuvre*. And there is always the chance of seeing them coming out of the house, walking the streets, always together, always besuited, always looking like 1970s' bank clerks, every sighting probably part of the performance art they have turned their lives into.

Gilbert and George are the Italian Gilbert Proesch and George Charles Ernestine Passmore from Flete, Plymouth. They bought no. 12 when the area was at its lowest ebb. 'It was like walking into a book in the 19th century: amazing light, and few people in the street,' according to Gilbert. They were the first to restore a house on Fournier Street. Around were button-making workshops, furriers and hat-makers – all now gone, though the buildings remain. Decades later they found that their locale had become one of the most fashionable places in central London.

The local street art often honours them. One graffito read *I would wallop Gilbert but not George*. The duo say 'We made an image out of it. Our favourite one featured the world's most famous words: prostitute, breast, penis, arse. It's the closest thing to freedom of speech you can get.'

To add to the mystique, the duo are ardent royalists, citing Prince Harry as a 'great model for many young people. He's highly trained.' They are also fervent Tories. One journalist visiting their home was shocked to find a poster of now former Tory prime minister David Cameron on the wall. After all, no artist could really be a Conservative, could they?

Address 8 Fournier Street, Spitalfields E1 6QE | Getting there Overground to Shoreditch High Street | Hours Viewable from the outside only | Tip Fournier Street is like a living museum. No. 3 was used as a hairdresser's in the 1992 Neil Jordan film *The Crying Game*. At no. 5 until recently was the Market Café, where Gilbert and George breakfasted for 30 years, even being known to remove their jackets when the temperature climbed above 95°. No. 12 is the duo's studio. No. 14 is a 1726 weaver's house where the silk for Queen Victoria's coronation gown was woven.

40 __ Grave of Alfred Linnell

Last resting place of a symbolic socialist martyr

Alfred Linnell was a young, radical legal clerk caught up in a demonstration on 20 November, 1887 in Trafalgar Square that was broken up with such violence by the police it became known as Bloody Sunday, just like a similar demo the week before. Ironically, the second demonstration had been called to protest against the police's heavy-handed tactics from the week before.

At one point the mounted police charged, and people panicked and fled. Linnell was struck down by a police horse and his neck broken under its hooves. He was left to lie in agony, even though a police ambulance was nearby. He was taken to hospital and died 12 days later.

The Times was not sympathetic to the demonstrators. 'It was no serious conviction of any kind, and no honest purpose that animated these howling toughs. It was simple love of disorder.' A rather differing account of events came from people like the artist Walter Crane. 'I never saw anything more like real warfare in my life – only the attack was all on one side.'

For the funeral at Tower Hamlets Cemetery on 18 December, thousands joined the procession in what the historian E. P. Thompson described as 'the greatest united demonstration which London had seen.' It was dusk by the time the crowd reached the cemetery. Speeches were read by lamplight. Even though few of the crowd knew Alfred Linnell, they hailed him, in the words of the leading Victorian intellectual, William Morris, as 'our brother and our friend.' Morris read the eulogy and advocated a 'holy war to prevent London from being turned into a huge prison.'

William Morris and Walter Crane designed a pamphlet in response to Linnell's death and to help raise money for his orphaned children, his wife having died, which read: 'Alfred Linnell, killed in Trafalgar Square, November 20, 1887: a Death Song.'

ALFRED LINNELL
1846-1887

Alfred Linnell, 1846 - 1887, is buried near this spot

On Sunday 13th November 1887,
ten thousand people marched towards Trafalgar Square,
protesting against repression in Ireland and unemployment.
Police and troops beat them with truncheons.

A week after 'Bloody Sunday',
Alfred Linnell, joined a gathering in Trafalgar Square
to protest against the authorities' violence.
He was knocked down by a police horse and died on December 2nd.

*Not one, not one, nor thousands must they slay
But one and all if they would dusk the day*

William Morris

Address Tower Hamlets Cemetery, Southern Grove, Bow E3 4PX | **Getting there** Underground to Bow Road (District and Hammersmith & City lines); bus 25, 205 or 425 | **Hours** Accessible 24 hours | **Tip** Other famous graves in this cemetery include that of Charles Jamrach, who supplied animals to the American showman P. T. Barnum, and Clara Grant OBE, the social reformer known as the 'Bundle Woman of Bow'.

41 — *Great Eastern* Launch Ramp

Launch site for the world's greatest ship

Wooden slats by the Thames in Millwall, once one of Britain's greatest shipbuilding areas, are the remains of the launch ramp for the mid-19th-century *Great Eastern* ship. When finished in 1857 it was the largest vessel the world had ever seen – and the first to be built out of metal.

The *Great Eastern* was designed by Isambard Kingdom Brunel and could take up to 6,000 passengers on a 22,500-mile route to Australia and back. It weighed 22,500 tons, one ton for each mile. Work began at Napier's Yard in spring 1854. The ship would be launched sideways into the river as Brunel feared that otherwise it might hurtle down the slipway with such force it could crash into the opposite bank.

The launch date was set for 3 November, 1857. Brunel wanted a low-key launch. Nevertheless, thousands turned up. No one knew what would be the official name, although *Great Eastern* was the favourite. Then Henry Thomas Hope, the major fundraiser, announced 'I christen this ship *Leviathan*' and … nothing happened. The beast refused to move! The press ridiculed Brunel, who organised another launch. And another. After three more aborted attempts the vessel, now renamed the *Great Eastern* was finally waterborne on 31 January, 1858. By then the owners had gone bankrupt.

The maiden voyage was a disaster as well. There was a huge explosion just past Hastings. Five stokers died after being scalded by hot steam. The ship was repaired, worked as a passenger liner between Britain and North America for a few years, and was then converted to cable-laying, setting the first transatlantic line in 1866. The ship's last days were spent running up and down the Mersey advertising Liverpool's Lewis' store. When it was broken up, two skeletons were found entombed between the double hull. A shipwright and his apprentice had been trapped during construction and starved to death.

Address Just east of Napier Avenue by the River Thames, Millwall E14 3QB | Getting there Mudchute DLR | Hours Accessible 24 hours | Tip Nothing else of note remains of industrial Millwall, only the docks, L-shaped Millwall Outer and Inner Docks, which occupy a huge part of the centre of the island.

42___Greenway

Eco-friendly walkway atop a sewer

New York has the High Line, Paris the Promenade Plantée; London has a lengthy lawn on top of a sewer. To many, the Greenway is the real eastern boundary of the East End, the people's boundary. The Greenway is a seven-mile path with an astonishing and ever-changing array of views, offering tantalising glimpses of the communities and structures beyond, used daily by thousands walking, trekking, biking, perambulating its route, and linking several green-friendly spaces in the industrialised parts at the edge of the East End.

Prosaically, the Greenway is simply the top of the Northern Outfall Sewer, designed by legendary engineer Joseph Bazalgette after the cholera outbreak of 1853 as part of his 82 miles of enclosed underground brick main sewers in the capital to rid the streets of raw sewage, this one carrying its effluence through gravity. Hence its nickname 'Sewerbank'.

The Greenway begins at the Hackney end off Wick Lane, at the wonderfully named Fish Island (see ch. 35). Hackney Wick has a little-known history. The world's first synthetic plastic, parkesine, was manufactured here. It was also where Eton public school ran a mission from 1913 to 1967 to better the lives of east Londoners through sport.

The Greenway then heads south-east and crosses the River Lea just south of Old Ford Locks. Once it's past the Lea there are staggering sightings of the London stadium, now home to West Ham United, and the ArcelorMittal *Orbit* comes into view (see ch. 4). More rivers appear – tributaries of the Lea with exotic names such as the City Mill River and Waterworks River – and the path then undercuts the busy A118, the main road connecting Bow and Stratford, heading out of the East End, through Plaistow and East Ham towards Beckton Alps in what is known as the Quietway. The sewer arrives at the Thames by Barking Creek, east of the delightfully named Cyprus.

Address From Victoria Park in the west to Beckton Alps in the east | Getting there
Pudding Mill Lane DLR | Hours Accessible 24 hours | Tip Just outside the East End and
east of the Olympic Park, by the Greenway, is Joseph Bazalgette's astonishing Byzantine
fantasy, Abbey Mills Pumping Station, nicknamed the 'Cathedral of Sewage'.

43 Huguenot Shadows

Traces of the East End's French community

A sundial on the Fournier Street side of the Jamme Masjid mosque, formerly a church and a synagogue, states in Latin *Umbra sumus* – 'we are shadows'. It is an elegant reminder of Huguenot East End, as are the magnificent merchant silk weavers' houses further along.

The Huguenots were French Protestants fleeing persecution in the late 16th century. They settled in Spitalfields by the ruins of the sacked priory, and when James I took the English throne in 1603 he boosted the silk trade by planting mulberry trees to rear silk worms. By the end of the century more than 20,000 East Enders were engaged in the silk trade.

Fournier Street off Brick Lane is not only a link with the days of silk weaving. It is also one of the most glorious streets in London, lined with houses built for silk merchants in the 18th century. Some of the properties sport wooden spools outside as a reminder of the traditional trades. At no. 2 is the Minister's House, designed by the master London church builder Nicholas Hawksmoor, alongside his celebrated Christ Church. No. 4, from 1726, incorporates England's first mahogany staircase, and brackets carved with ears of wheat and scallop shells. At no. 14 is Howard House where the silk used for Queen Victoria's coronation gown was woven. These houses were saved by devout campaigning in the 1970s led by squatters and championed by historians such as Dan Cruikshank, who lives locally.

The Huguenots also pioneered new forms of eating. Their idea of combining fried fish with pieces of potato, also fried, became the quintessentially English 'fish and chips'. It took a few generations for the Huguenots to lose their ethnic trappings. French Protestant churches were converted to English Protestant churches. Family names were anglicised. Lenoir became Black; Blanc, White; de la Neuve Maison, Newhouse. Some names, such as Farage, remain unchanged.

Address Fournier Street, Spitalfields E1 6QE | Getting there Overground to Shoreditch High Street | Hours Accessible 24 hours | Tip It's not just Fournier Street that captures the glorious Georgian gestalt. It is part of a small but sturdy estate to the north of similar stretches, including Princelet, Wilkes and Elder streets.

44 Immigrants' Landing Stage
How immigrants entered London before air travel

Hundreds of thousands of immigrants entered London over the centuries at Irongate Stairs, a landing stage by the Thames where Tower Bridge now looms over the site. Many were East European Jews who travelled in dreadful conditions on herring boats, herded in the hold in near darkness.

Until passports were introduced in 1914 there was no legislation preventing immigrants entering the country. At Hamburg, unscrupulous racketeers would charge one mark for passage to London, two marks to New York, and then turf off those who had paid the higher fare at London rather than bother taking them on the considerably longer journey.

Some 100,000 Jews arrived in the East End here after the 1881 assassination of the Russian Czar was blamed on them. Many of the new arrivals would immediately be whisked off to Schewzik's Russian Vapour Baths on Brick Lane – 'Best Massage in London: Invaluable relief for Rheumatism, Gout, Sciatica, Neuritis, Lumbago and Allied Complaints.' Ironically, the Jewish immigrants met hostility from Jewish welfare groups who had written to their counterparts in Eastern Europe pleading with 'all right-thinking persons among our brethren in Germany, Russia and Austria to place a barrier to the flow of foreigners, to persuade these voyagers not to venture to come to a land they know nothing about. It is better that they live a life of sorrow in their native place than bear the shame of famine and perish in a strange land.'

Of the many immigrants, the most celebrated has to be Józef Korzeniowski, Ukrainian, but not Jewish. Although he did not master English until his twenties, he later wrote some of the greatest works of English literature as Joseph Conrad, whose terrifying *Heart of Darkness*, which begins on the Thames further east, presaged the horrors of the 20th century and was turned into the equally powerful film *Apocalypse Now*.

Address Tower Bridge SE1 2UP | Getting there Underground to Tower Hill (Circle and District lines); Tower Gateway DLR; bus 42, 78 or 343 | Hours Accessible 24 hours | Tip Above, towering imperially over the river and filling the skyline, is Tower Bridge with its powerful Gothic towers, built in 1894, one of the most famous and memorable images of London, even if thousands of tourists regularly mistake it for London Bridge, a quarter of a mile west.

45 Isaac Rosenberg Plaque
Tribute to the East End's greatest artist-cum-poet

Born in Bristol to Lithuanian-Jewish parents in 1890, Isaac Rosenberg was raised in Stepney, on Cable Street no less, self-taught at Whitechapel Library and then more formally at the Slade School of Art. He became a gifted artist and one of the greatest World War I poets, dying in northern France in 1918.

By the age of 14, Rosenberg had decided 'That wealth, with its soul-crushing scourges placed into hands by fate/Hath made the cement of its towers, grim-girdled by our despair.' He joined the Whitechapel boys, members of the Socialist League, a time when the local MP, Major William Evans-Gordon, a member of the extreme nationalist British Brothers League, had described the Jewish immigrants as 'the off-scum of Europe.'

Thanks to three wealthy Jewish women Rosenberg accidentally met, he was able to attend the Slade where he met other major talents such as David Bomberg and Stanley Spencer. Always impoverished, Rosenberg enlisted in the British Army in 1916. Unlike his fellow war poets, Wilfred Owen and Siegfried Sassoon, Rosenberg was not an officer but a private – in the 12th Bantam Battalion of the Suffolk Regiment – and could only write from the trenches, rather than an officer's underground shelter:

'Down – a shell – O! Christ,/I am choked … safe … dust blind, I/See trench floor poppies/Strewn. Smashed you lie.'

He hated the war, and in a letter admitted 'I never joined the army for patriotic reasons. Nothing can justify war. I suppose we must all fight to get the trouble over.' Early in 1918, Rosenberg applied for a transfer to the British Army's Jewish Battalion fighting in Mesopotamia, but before he could move he was killed aged 27, his body never recovered from the mud of the Somme. Rosenberg's self-portraits hang in the National Portrait Gallery and Tate Britain. He is the only Jew commemorated in Westminster Abbey's Poets' Corner.

Address Whitechapel Gallery, 77–82 Whitechapel High Street, Whitechapel E1 7QX |
Getting there Underground to Aldgate East (District and Hammersmith & City lines) |
Hours Plaque accessible 24 hours; gallery Tue–Sun 11am–6pm, Thu until 9pm | **Tip**
Whitechapel Gallery is the most revered in the country east of the art houses of the West
End. In 1939 it displayed Picasso's anti-war epic *Guernica*. The groundbreaking pop-art
exhibition *This is Tomorrow* was held here in 1956. Two years later it showcased the first
major exhibition of Jackson Pollock works in the country.

46 Island Gardens

Sensational view at the tip of the Isle of Dogs

No one had heard of Island Gardens until the Docklands Light Railway opened in 1987. Now crowds flock to this no longer inaccessible part of Cubitt Town to see the majestic view of Christopher Wren's Royal Naval Palace across the water, one of the most spectacular waterside sights in the country, as captured by Canaletto in his 1752 painting *Greenwich Hospital from the North Bank of the Thames.*

A strange sight here is the Edwardian dome of the underwater foot passage linking the area with Greenwich. Until the DLR was built, this was the only access to the South, and using it was an event in itself, what with the stairs and the seemingly never-ending route of the tunnel itself. In the 1970s, a regular user was a budding young pianist, Julian (Jools) Holland, making his way to The Great Eastern pub (1 Glenaffric Avenue) where he had a stint.

The pub, then known as the Waterman's Arms, had a reputation and crowds flocked here, although those arriving by car would be tested by the local urchins' request to 'mind your car for ten bob, guv'nor.' It was all down to the unlikely landlord: the social gadfly and writer Daniel Farson: 'Photographer, writer, and drunk. Mythomanic, egotist,' as his obituary in *The Independent* in 1997 described him. Farson was a man with a past. In the mid-1930s he had accompanied his broadcaster father James on an assignment to Germany and been patted on the head by no less than Adolf Hitler, who praised him as a 'good Aryan boy'. Farson remodelled the pub as an old-fashioned music hall and attracted a reasonably interesting retinue of visitors not usually seen in the East End: Clint Eastwood, Brian Epstein, Judy Garland and Shirley Bassey.

In 1979, one of the greatest scenes in British film history was shot here: Bob Hoskins in *The Long Good Friday* ordering Nick Stringer to 'walk to the car, Billy, or I'll blow your spine off.'

Address Island Gardens, Cubitt Town E14 | Getting there Island Gardens DLR; bus 135, D 7 | Hours Accessible 24 hours | Tip Trying to find any pub in this, the old-fashioned working-class ungentrified part of the Isle of Dogs, is a task. However, The Ship at 290 Westferry Road, close to where Brunel didn't manage to launch the *Great Eastern* properly, fits the bill.

47 Isle of Dogs

Magnificent, mysterious, now clearly capitalist

The very name of this U-shaped peninsula, jutting into the Thames for one and half miles north–south and half a mile east–west, captures a mystique that has long intrigued people.

Where did the name come from? It might be a corruption of Isle of Ducks, which changed when Charles I placed the royal kennels here. In mediaeval times it was barren, forlorn, unpopulated and reachable only by boat. It flooded easily. When the diarist Samuel Pepys visited in 1665 he wrote 'so we were fain to stay there, in the unlucky Isle of Dogs, in a chill place, the night cold, to our great discomfort.' Everything changed at the end of the 18th century. With the growth in river-borne trade, the authorities built here massive docks. The first, West India Dock, opened in 1802. It took imports from the West Indies such as rum and sugar. As the century proceeded, the 'island', as locals called it, became the hub of London industry. It was Planet Vulcan, a burning smithy of iron and steel powering shipbuilding and engineering, sound-tracked by the hiss of steam and the clang of metal on metal. Around these were built streets of tiny basic terraced housing, a pub on practically every corner. By the 1980s it had all gone. The docks had shut, much of the housing had been replaced by grim tower blocks, the life sucked out of the island.

Then everything changed again, mostly in the island's north-west Canary Wharf enclave. Monumental regeneration. A new city of gleaming glass and granite skyscrapers, the tallest in the country, sprang up as finance houses and newspaper offices moved east. These created the 21st-century Isle of Dogs, a bastion of conspicuous wealth around the old West India and Millwall docks, linked by a serpentine light railway system and ultra-fast tube into central London, yet in the shadow of the deprived estates that still line large parts of the island.

Address E14 | Getting there Underground to Canary Wharf (Jubilee line); various DLR stops | Hours Accessible 24 hours | Tip More than a third of the land mass is actually water – in various Millwall and West India docks that fill the centre. Few remnants of the old industrial Isle of Dogs and its Victorian houses remain, the best being the constables' cottages on Garford Street at the north-west corner of the island.

48_Jack London's Abyss

East End home of fin-de-siècle *writer*

What was Ye Frying Pan pub, one of many such surviving buildings on Brick Lane where now there are no pubs, was the lodging place of the great American writer Jack London when he visited the East End to write his eye-opening and horrifying *The People of the Abyss* in 1902.

At that time, the impoverished and bedraggled conditions of the area were at their most acute. He could find 'No more dreary spectacle on this earth. The colour of life is gray and drab. Everything is helpless, hopeless, unrelieved, and dirty. The people are dirty, short of stature, and of wretched or beer-sodden appearance. Strange, vagrant odours come drifting along the greasy wind, and the rain, when it falls, is more like grease than water from heaven.'

When the writer first informed friends in respectable, suburban Highbury Vale three miles north that he intended visiting the East End they told him: 'You can't do it, you know. You had better see the police for a guide.' Undeterred, he headed for travel firm Thomas Cook in the City of London. There he discovered they were keener on Darkest Africa than the Stygian wastes of Stepney. An assistant begged the American not to attempt the journey. 'We are not accustomed to taking travellers to the East End; we receive no call to take them there, and we know nothing whatsoever about the place at all. It is so – hem – so unusual.'

Among his many remarkable encounters east of Aldgate, London recalled Saturday night bath night in the Whitechapel workhouse where the men entered the communal basin in pairs. When they got out another pair jumped in, the water remaining unchanged, even though, as the writer pointed out, one man's back was 'a mass of blood from attacks of vermin and retaliatory scratching.'

The People of the Abyss was London's favourite. 'Of all my books, [it is] the one I love most. No other work of mine contains as much of my heart.'

Address 13 Brick Lane, Spitalfields E1 6PU | **Getting there** Underground to Aldgate East (District and Hammersmith & City lines) | **Hours** Accessible 24 hours | **Tip** A walk up and down the length of Brick Lane reveals almost a dozen Victorian buildings that were clearly once pubs but have long since found an alternative use. The only local pub now is The Pride of Spitalfields at 3 Heneage Street, just a few yards off Brick Lane.

49 Jack the Ripper Wall

Much visited site at the heart of Ripper mystery

Every night of the year hundreds of curious sightseers, many on guided tours, fired up by the legend and myth of Jack the Ripper, flock here to see a location connected with one of the most fascinating aspects relating to the grim, gripping story.

On the night of 30 September, 1888, following two gruesome murders of prostitutes locally over the previous few weeks, two more murders took place within hours of each other. Elizabeth Stride, a 45-year-old Swedish woman, was found with her throat cut, the blood still pouring out, on Berner Street, St George's. An hour later another prostitute, Catherine Eddowes, was killed on Mitre Square, near Aldgate station, half a mile away.

Eddowes' white apron was torn during the attack and part of the garment was dropped here on Goulston Street. There it was found by a policeman who, looking up at the wall (currently inaccessible, to obstruct gawpers), saw graffiti proclaiming: *The Juwes are not the men that will be blamed for nothing*. Fearful of a pogrom against the Jews, the police wiped the message.

Hundreds of books, articles and websites have attempted to explain the graffito. Most fail to realise it simply comes from ancient Freemasonry. In Masonic symbolism, the 'Juwes' are the three assassins, Jubela, Jubelo and Jubelum, who in the year 959 BC killed Hiram Abiff, the architect of Solomon's Temple (the key building in Masonic lore) after he refused to reveal to them the secret names of God. When the three were caught, they were put to death, their throats cut from ear to ear, 'their breasts torn open,' their entrails thrown over the shoulder – just as the five victims of Jack the Ripper were killed.

Three days before the night of the double murder someone, possibly the murderer, had written a letter to the Central News Agency claiming responsibility for the killings and using the name Jack the Ripper.

Address Goulston Street, Aldgate E1 7TP | Getting there Underground to Aldgate East (District and Hammersmith & City lines) | Hours Accessible 24 hours | Tip Mary Kelly, the Ripper's last victim, was murdered a couple of hundred yards north in a now demolished property by the corner of Brushfield Street and Commercial Street. A number of the victims and friends drank in The Ten Bells pub opposite.

50 Jewish East End
Ghostly traces of a vanished community

No one knows exactly when the first Jews settled in the East End. Most sources cite how Jews from Rouen, northern France, came with William the Conqueror after 1066 to help with the economy, coinage and diamond trading. Yet a piece of stone found in a Roman site on what is now Mark Lane, Aldgate, shows a relief of Samson and the foxes from the Old Testament. As the Romans were then pagans there must have been Jews in east London in the first century AD.

In 1290, after 200 years of often volatile and vicarious acceptance among the gentile community, Edward I expelled the Jews from England. When Oliver Cromwell became Lord Protector of England in the 1650s he invited Jewish bankers and merchants back, to settle in London. By 1800 there were about 10,000 Jews in the capital, mostly in the East End. They sold second-hand clothes, fruit, birds, shells, knives and razors. Most professions were then barred to them. Jews were ridiculed as misers, usurers, cheats, coin-clippers, pimps and thieves – like Dickens' Fagin. Such deleterious descriptions intensified when hordes of East European Jews fleeing persecution at the end of the 19th century arrived. The *East London Observer* was openly contemptuous and demanded their exclusion from the neighbourhood: 'They depreciate our home products and depress our markets. Their low state of civilisation tends to demoralise whole populations of native workers.' The existing Jewish community was also horrified by the arrival of the East European immigrants and strove to anglicise them: 'We may not be able to make them rich but we may hope to render them English in feeling and conduct.'

Gentile hostility culminated in the Battle of Cable Street of 1936 (see ch. 16). After World War II, most East End Jews moved to the more salubrious suburbs. Now there's little left of the Jewish East End but survivals like this seem even more remarkable.

Address Brune Street, Spitalfields E1 7NJ | **Getting there** Underground (Central, Circle and Hammersmith & City lines) and National Rail to Liverpool Street; bus 242 | **Hours** Accessible 24 hours | **Tip** A few hundred yards to the west on Sandys Row is that rarity nowadays – an East End synagogue. It was built as a church in 1766 by Huguenots and bought by a Jewish society, *Hevrat Menac'hem Avalim C'hesed v'Emes*, 'The Comforters of Mourners Kindness and Truth Society' a hundred years later.

51 John Williams' Makeshift Grave

Terrifying burial for innocent murder suspect

John Williams, accused of the infamous local Ratcliffe Highway murders of 1811, was found hanged before he could be tried. His corpse was then paraded through the East End streets until it reached this crossroads of Cable Street and Cannon Street Road where it was thrown into a pit, a stake driven through the heart, as was done to suicides in those days. But was Williams guilty in the first place?

The Ratcliffe Highway murders occurred near London's most violent street in 1811. The first killings took place on Sunday 8 December when draper Timothy Marr at no. 29 sent his maid to buy some late supper oysters. When she returned, and failed to get an answer to her knocks, she secured help. Inside were Mr and Mrs Marr, their baby son, and the shop boy freshly dead.

On Thursday 19 December, a crowd of people watched at the nearby King's Arms pub as the lodger, Turner, frantically made his way out of the window using knotted sheets crying: 'Murder! Murder! … they are murdering the people in the house!' Inside, the landlord, his wife and their maid were slain. A John Williams, who had once sailed with Timothy Marr, was arrested after a tip-off. His trial was a farce but before a verdict could be reached he was found dead in Coldbath prison. Historians now believe he was eliminated for reasons unknown and the motive for the killings remains a mystery although some have linked its Masonic aspects with the more infamous later Masonic Jack the Ripper killings.

In 1911, on the centenary of the burial, workmen dug Williams up. A criminologist took his arm while the owner of the pub at the corner kept the skull as a souvenir. The skull was later stolen by an occultist trying to create a golem, an artificial human being made according to mystical Hebrew ritual.

Address Junction of Cable Street and Cannon Street Road, St George's E1 0BH | Getting there Overground to Shadwell | Hours Accessible 24 hours | Tip At nearby 12 Cable Street stands the highly controversial Jack the Ripper Museum, which incidentally doesn't feature the most plausible explanation for the crimes. Its opening in 2015 was greeted with protestors and a denunciation from the council.

52 London Stadium

East London's Wembley, not without its detractors

Monumental iconic statement or white elephant, the London Stadium is the centrepiece of the remarkable and epic redevelopment of Stratford at the eastern border of the East End that also includes the Queen Elizabeth Park, Velodrome, Aquatics Centre and the monstrous ArcelorMittal *Orbit*. The stadium was built for the 2012 Olympics but is now mostly used as the home of perennially unsuccessful football club West Ham United.

Preparation began in 2007 after London was surprisingly awarded the games at the expense of Paris. The alternative, to upgrade Wembley, was rejected so that this run-down tract of east London could be redeveloped. Railway sidings and light industrial depots were wiped out, and the multitude of tributaries of the River Lea tamed and rerouted. Philip Johnson for Populous designed a stadium able to hold 80,000. It won a Royal Institute of British Architects award, but architecture critics were underwhelmed, especially when comparing it to Beijing's Olympic Bird's Nest, built for 2008.

The London Olympics began with a most exciting opening ceremony, topped with the supposed arrival of the queen and James Bond into the stadium by parachute from a helicopter. The highlight of the Games saw David Rudisha of Kenya set a world record for the 800 metres and Mo Farah win the 10,000 metres final.

With the Olympics over, the original legacy plan was to convert the stadium to hold 25,000–30,000 for athletics. When it was announced that, instead, West Ham United were to be the main tenants, there was uproar, especially from those who pointed out how football's riches should be able to take care of the sport and that West Ham had a perfectly acceptable and much-loved stadium in Upton Park. The stadium now also puts on concerts and other sports such as baseball and cricket, even though spectators are unimpressed at the distance between the seats and the action.

Address London Stadium, Queen Elizabeth Olympic Park E20 2ST | Getting there Underground (Central and Jubilee lines), DLR, Overground and National Rail to Stratford | Hours Outside, accessible 24 hours; inside only for events. Tours daily 10am–3pm except match days | Tip Half a mile north is the 6,000-seater velodrome for cycling where Chris Hoy and Sarah Storey starred during the 2012 Games. It is the first venue in the world offering four types of cycling: track cycling, road racing, BMX and mountain biking.

53 London's Hospital

Casualty, cockpits and curios at ancient infirmary

If you're going to get ill in the East End, then the best place to recover must be the Royal London Hospital, a major emergency centre that occupies a huge site opposite Whitechapel station and boasts of one of the longest histories in the area.

The hospital was founded in 1740 and moved here from a site nearer the Tower in 1757. It was here that Thomas Barnardo, founder of the charity of the same name, underwent his medical training in 1866 and where John Merrick, the 'Elephant Man', lived in the 1880s after being rescued from a freak show at 159 Whitechapel Road and where he taught himself to read using the Bible. Indeed, the Elephant Man's remains are kept in the hospital museum, which is not open to the public. In 1889, shortly after the spate of local murders now associated with Jack the Ripper abated, the building housed an exhibition displaying waxwork models of the victim's bodies. A few years later, a new trainee nurse was Edith Cavell who, during the Great War, helped some 200 Allied soldiers escape from German-occupied Belgium.

Because of its East End location, the hospital's casualty wing has often tended injured villains. Eric Mason, a member of the Kray twins' firm, believed to be the last man to be flogged in prison, was thrown out of a car outside the hospital in 1965 wrapped in a blanket having been sacked from the Kray gang with a £40 'redundancy' payment.

A major feature of the hospital is its helipad operated by London's Air Ambulance, whose vehicles are based at the other side of the capital at RAF Northolt. From the hospital, the chopper can reach any patient inside the M25 within an astonishing 15 minutes, perfect for serious RTAs, industrial accidents and incidents on the railway. As the hospital has recently expanded south, the section behind the well-known façade fronting Whitechapel Road is being converted into council offices.

Address Whitechapel Road, east of New Road, Whitechapel E1 1FR | Getting there Underground (District and Hammersmith & City lines) and Overground to Whitechapel | Hours Accessible 24 hours | Tip John Merrick, the 'Elephant Man', was kept in a cage in the window of the shop at nearby 159 Whitechapel Road in 1884 and made to act like a dog to entice people inside to see a freak show. Merrick was rescued from his plight by Dr Treves, a specialist in skin disorders, who took him to the London Hospital.

54 Mark Gertler Memorial

Tribute to a little-known Bloomsbury group member

A roundel set in the pavement at 32 Elder Street, Spitalfields, marks the house where the early 20th-century artist Mark Gertler lived. It shows a detail from his painting *The Merry-Go-Round* (1916), once described by D. H. Lawrence as 'the best modern picture I have seen,' and now in Tate Britain.

Gertler was born Marks Gertler to Polish-Jewish immigrants in 1891. On leaving school in 1906 he enrolled in art classes at Regent Street Polytechnic but dropped out after a year through lack of funds. Two years later he finished third in a national art competition. This led him to apply for a scholarship from the Jewish Education Aid Society to resume his studies. He was successful and enrolled at the Slade. There he met Paul Nash, Stanley Spencer and a fellow child of immigrant Jews, the ill-fated Isaac Rosenberg. He also fell obsessively in love with bohemian socialite Dora Carrington, but his desire remained unrequited, as she had declared her love for the biographer Lytton Strachey, a founding member of the Bloomsbury Group. Equally unrequited was the homosexual love Edward Marsh, Churchill's private secretary, had for Gertler.

But Gertler did find a patron in Lady Ottoline Morrell, another wealthy Bloomsbury Group socialite. To the author Virginia Woolf, the main figure in the Bloomsbury Group, Gertler was incorrigible. 'Good God, what an egoist! But he is a forcible young man; if limited, able and respectable within those limits; as hard as a cricket ball.' He was characterised as Loerke in D. H. Lawrence's *Women in Love* (1920) and Gombauld in Aldous Huxley's *Crome Yellow* (1921).

In 1920, Gertler was diagnosed with TB and incarcerated in a sanatorium. In 1939, he gassed himself in his London studio during a bout of depression brought on by poverty, critical derision from an exhibition, Carrington's own suicide and fears over the imminent world war.

Address 32 Elder Street, Spitalfields E1 6BT | Getting there Overground to Shoreditch High Street; bus 242 | Hours House viewable from the outside only | Tip The Spitalfields Trust acquired other Elder Street properties, 1725-built nos. 5–7, in 1977 so that its saving could catalyse the restoration of the area. The battle was on to stop the council's 'bookending' demolition – starting at one end and thereby spoiling the adjacent property which would then have to be demolished. It worked.

55 Meridian Line

Imaginary line that divides the planet

The Meridian Line or 0 degrees longitude divides the world into east and west, much as the Equator does the same north–south, and it runs right through the East End in Poplar. The Meridian Line measures approximately 12,400 miles and connects the North and South Poles. Its main function is to set time, Greenwich Mean Time, around the world. Similar lines, radiating from Pole to Pole, circling the Earth, similarly set time through their locale.

The Greeks set the first Meridian. The word comes from the Spanish *meridies*, meaning 'midday'. Greenwich, on the opposite bank of the Thames, was chosen for the setting of the British-inspired Meridian Line as it was the home of the long-standing Royal Observatory, where the 18th-century carpenter and clockmaker John Harrison became the first individual to find a way of measuring time at sea. Countries across the world eventually realised that an agreed single Meridian was needed, as France and Sweden each had their own.

An international conference was held in Washington DC in 1884. France wanted Paris to be chosen, but Greenwich won the vote by 22 votes to 1. Only the Dominican Republic voted against. The French agreed to accept London, grudgingly, as long as the United Kingdom agreed to adopt the metric system immediately, something that still hasn't taken place.

The Meridian Line joins the East End right by the Thames, in the much-redeveloped East India Docks area, with an ambitious display of street art on Prime Meridian Walk, just west of Jamestown Way, that consists of a long silver line on the pavement. As for its presence in other parts of the East End, further north it crosses Saffron Avenue and East India Dock where, one assumes, most locals are unaware that they are striding across the two halves of the Earth, before heading out of the East End over Bow Creek, the East End's eastern boundary.

Address Prime Meridian Walk, Poplar E14 2AB | Getting there East India DLR | Hours
Accessible 24 hours | Tip A short journey on the DLR south of the Thames leads to the
Royal Observatory itself and exhibitions on the Meridian.

56 Mile End Road Mural

Remarkable street art on a wall

Painted by Canadian Mychael Barratt, whose Huguenot ancestors first came to the East End 300 years ago as refugees, over six weeks in the summer of 2011, the mural was devised after local law firm T. V. Edwards were refused planning permission for a large advert on the side of their building. One of the partners saw Barratt's work in Blackfriars and a commission followed.

The mural takes some studying, and features some of the most famous and remarkable figures who have come to the East End:

George Bernard Shaw, who would meet with the local Fabian Society on Whitechapel Road; William Booth who began the Salvation Army locally; Antipodean explorer James Cook lived at 88 Mile End Road when not at sea; Prince Monolulu, an excitable horse-racing tipster, who frequented Petticoat Lane where he was famous for his clarion call: 'I gotta horse!'; Frederick Charrington of the famous brewing family who forsook his inheritance to preach temperance, depicted here with a dray horse; Vladimir Lenin, who planned revolution in the early 20th century at the socialist club on the corner of Fulbourne Street and Whitechapel Road; Joseph Merrick, the tragic Elephant Man whose remains are at the London Hospital in Whitechapel; Mahatma Gandhi, who stayed in Bow in 1931 when he came to London to discuss Indian independence; Samuel Pepys who visited the Mile End Road, as he recalled in his diary; gifted local artists Isaac Rosenberg and Mark Gertler; Edith Cavell, who trained as a nurse at London Hospital before working in Belgium during the Great War; gangster twins Reggie and Ronnie Kray; Gilbert and George, kings of Spitalfields; the awe-inspiring Christ Church, Spitalfields, designed by Nicholas Hawksmoor; the award-winning but sadly demolished *House* by Rachel Whiteread, which was simply a concrete cast of the inside of a house temporarily placed on Grove Road, Mile End.

Address 35–37 Mile End Road, Bethnal Green E1 4TP | Getting there Underground to Stepney Green (District and Hammersmith & City lines) or Whitechapel (District, Circle and Hammersmith & City lines) | Hours Accessible 24 hours | Tip A mile north, the wall of the Lord Morpeth pub at 402 Old Ford Road, Bow, displays a giant mural of Sylvia Pankhurst, Britain's greatest 20th-century political campaigner, who campaigned with local suffragettes around the time of the Great War.

57 Millwall FC's Origins

Notorious football club's humble origins

'Millwall'. The very name has become a metonym for everything that represents a different kind of football; proper working-class, pie-and-pint, pre-Premier League puffery and pseudery football. Sadly, the name has also become indelibly associated with regular outbreaks of football hooliganism, despite all the noble efforts the club has made to eradicate the vice among their own supporters.

Even though Millwall FC has played in south London in South Bermondsey for over a hundred years, the area called Millwall is very much in the East End, occupying the western half of the Isle of Dogs. To complete the paradox, Canary Wharf, the essence of the capital's 21st-century conspicuous capitalism, as far removed from the area's industrial and dock origins as possible, is in Millwall, a factette possibly lost on the tens of thousands who work there.

Millwall Football Club was founded in 1885 as Millwall Rovers by workers at the since demolished local Morton's food factory. Morton's made a variety of successful foodstuffs. Their bloater fish paste was particularly popular with cats and dogs. Many of the workers and the team were Scottish, so they chose the national colours of blue and white, and the Scottish rampant lion as their symbol. Their first ground was where the smart Cascades tower block now stands. Millwall Rovers then played on Glengall Road, now Tiller Road, and temporarily by the mudchute, the dumping ground for the stinking mud dredged from the docks, which proved to be an excellent breeding ground for diphtheria.

The players often changed at the Lord Nelson pub, and occasionally played in the field behind. Games would start at 3.15pm, rather than the normal 3pm, to allow dockers to get to the game after their shift. Millwall Rovers soon became simply Millwall and played at a variety of Isle of Dogs' grounds before crossing the Thames in 1910.

Address The Lord Nelson, 1 Manchester Road, Cubitt Town E14 3BD, +44 (0)207 987 1970 |
Getting there Island Gardens DLR; bus 277 or D7 to East Ferry Road | Hours Sun–Thu
noon–11pm, Fri & Sat noon–midnight | Tip A few hundred yards south is the Ferry House,
the oldest pub on the island, which dates back to 1722 and is even marked on Rocque's map of
1745, when the only other nearby feature was a gibbet.

58__Minnie Lansbury Clock

Tribute to suffragette and pioneering politician

A clock high on the wall of Electric House, Bow, pays tribute to the suffragette, pioneering Labour politician Minnie Lansbury, one of the first women to take a leading role in the burgeoning Labour Party, who was related to the celebrated Labour leader George Lansbury and the actress Angela Lansbury.

Minnie came from a Jewish family. Her father was a bootmaker and coal merchant. In 1914 she married Edgar Lansbury whose father, George, became leader of the Labour Party after Ramsay MacDonald, the first Labour premier, split the party in 1931. Minnie was a teacher and a member of the East London Federation of Suffragettes, founded by Britain's greatest political campaigner, Sylvia Pankhurst. She chaired the War Pensions Committee, fighting for the rights of widows and orphans wounded in the Great War, and worked with the Women's Freedom League, aimed at getting women the vote. In 1919 she was elected onto Poplar council. Two years later she was one of five women councillors jailed for six weeks for refusing to increase the rates in this, the poorest part of the East End, a campaign led by her father-in-law, George Lansbury. On her way to prison, she was quoted as saying, 'I wish the Government joy in its efforts to get this money from the people of Poplar. Poplar will pay its share of London's rates when Westminster, Kensington, and the City do the same.' Imprisonment didn't help her health. She caught pneumonia and died in 1922 aged only 33.

The clock on Electric House on Bow Road was erected in the 1930s. It was restored, and painted green and gold in 2008 through public appeal organised by the Jewish East End Celebration Society and the Heritage of London Trust. Angela Lansbury contributed to the cost. Minnie's name is one of 58 mentioned on the plinth of the statue of the moderate suffragist Millicent Fawcett in Parliament Square.

Address Electric House, Bow Road, Bow E3 2BL | Getting there Underground to Bow Road (District and Hammersmith & City lines) | Hours Accessible 24 hours | Tip A few hundred yards east on the same main road is Bromley Public Hall, where the first meeting of the East London Federation of Suffragettes took place on Valentine's Day 1913.

59 Mother Kelly's Doorstep

'Lingering all alone down Paradise Row'

This rare stretch of Georgian properties in a dishevelled corner of the East End, drowned out by the trains of the Liverpool Street line, has been captured for all time in one of the best-known East End songs: 'On Mother Kelly's Doorstep', the very mention of which elicits the famous follow-up… 'Down Paradise Row'. The song fits more into the tradition of east London music hall songs than the pop charts, the well-known lyrics continuing: 'I'd sit along o' Nelly/She'd sit along o' Joe/She's got a little hole in her frock/hole in her shoe/hole in her sock/where her toe peeped through.'

The song was written in 1925 by Alex Stephens about a real Mother Kelly, also known as Nelly Moss, itself adapted from Nelly Moses, a young Jewish immigrant from Lithuania, who lived on the cobbled-stone terrace at the end of the 19th century. In 1968, the cross-dressing performer Danny La Rue took the song to no. 33 in the charts before adopting it as his theme tune.

In 2012, Tower Hamlets council deferred an application for a four-storey hotel on the site, concerned that the new building would clash with the remaining Georgian town houses down Paradise Row and the Museum of Childhood opposite. Another surviving property on Paradise Row is the 18th-century home of the Jewish pugilist Daniel Mendoza, heavyweight champion 1792–95. Because boxers tended to give themselves memorable names, he billed himself as 'Mendoza the Jew'. His first fight was a victory against the equally-inspired named 'Harry the Coalheaver'.

It was in this house that Mendoza wrote *The Art of Boxing*, in which he advocated a scientific approach rather than the typically chaotic, coarse and claustrophobic style of the day. 'The ideas of coarseness and vulgarity which are naturally attached to the Science of Pugilism, will, I trust, be done away, by a candid perusal of the following pages.'

Address Paradise Row, Bethnal Green E2 9LE | Getting there Underground to Bethnal Green (Central line); bus 106 or 254 | Hours Accessible 24 hours | Tip Nearly two miles east, just off Mile End Road, lies Coborn Road. The street itself is unmemorable, but it was while chatting to a friend here in the early 1870s that Colin McCallum, an ambitious music hall star, decided to rebrand himself Charles Coborn, and in his new guise he went on to become a leading performer responsible for two landmark songs: 'Two Lovely Black Eyes' (1886) and 'The Man Who Broke the Bank at Monte Carlo' (1891).

60 Mudlark Beach

'Mud, mud, glorious mud'

What a thrill to descend a set of ancient steps that leads down to the river, following in the footsteps of thousands of pirates, smugglers and watermen, in the ultimate getting away from it all in the East End, to find a surprise and an unknown beach, and the flotsam and jetsam it yields.

The Thames' shore has always been the haunt of the mudlarks: explorers, investigators, searchers, sifting through the waterside debris to unearth lost treasure or mostly junk. A licence is needed in the 21st century; Dickens' characters didn't bother in *Our Mutual Friend*. Mudlarking is now a popular hobby, and the stretches of land hidden away behind the monstrous warehouses on Wapping High Street are the perfect places to indulge. The river yields much esoterica: china and Tudor clay pipes that belonged to the watermen who used the river as their litter bin; bones from tanneries; roof tiles dating back to the Great Fire of London; the shards of witch bottles used for curses. One woman found half a tin-glazed French Quimper plate but threw it back because it was too big, only to see it posted on another mudlarker's Instagram account later.

Two hundred years ago the mudlarks indulged not for leisure but necessity. These were children who scraped a living scavenging for items of value that could be sold. They were known as toshers and would wade through the mud, where the sewers emptied their contents, on the look-out for anything 'interesting' discharged along with the lavatorial contents. They had their pride, dressing in beautiful velveteen coats, but came equipped with a seven-foot pole to stymie the sewer rats.

If the shore doesn't yield treasure there's always the possibility of spotting a seal, a dolphin, or as in 2006, a young female Northern bottlenose whale, Diana, who journeyed all the way past Westminster to Albert Bridge before sadly dying from convulsions.

Address Pelican Stairs, next to the Prospect of Whitby pub, Wapping E1W 3SH | Getting
there Overground to Wapping; bus 100 | Hours Accessible 24 hours, although you need to
apply to the Port of London Authority for a permit | Tip Wapping needs a good chunk of
the day to explore properly. For a complete contrast to the damp and dank delights of the
river, head west to Wapping Pierhead and its glorious Georgian houses, where the captains
lived so close to the docks.

61 Museum's Prefab

Unusual origins of London's childhood museum

The Victoria and Albert Museum of Childhood in Bethnal Green is the largest institution of its kind in the world. Appropriately it is located in an area where child mortality was worryingly high in Victorian times and which nowadays has the highest rate of childhood deprivation in Britain. The museum's mission is 'to enable everyone, especially the young, to explore and enjoy the designed world, in particular objects made for and made by children.'

In 1851, the rising politician William Gladstone suggested a museum be built in Bethnal Green. Three leading local figures, the social reformer Sir Antonio Brady, the rector Reverend Septimus Hansard and a Dr Millar bought the land and lobbied Parliament for a museum to be built. In 1872, it was founded as the Bethnal Green Museum. This was a time of great progressive changes in education. In 1880, it would become compulsory for children aged up to 10 to go to school, and this coincided with the Victorian belief that people could improve their minds in their leisure time by visiting museums and galleries.

Meanwhile, in South Kensington, Prince Albert had created an estate of museums in the wake of the 1851 Great Exhibition, aimed at showing off Britain's technological and cultural prowess. The South Kensington Museum featured a simple iron frame covered in corrugated iron, nicknamed 'the Brompton boilers'. Benjamin Disraeli, the Tory politician, argued in Parliament that the structure could be reused, and so it was taken down in 1872 and moved eight miles east to Bethnal Green. The rest of the museum was designed in the German Rundbogenstil style by James William Wild. In the 1920s, it began to focus on exhibits for children, and in 1974 the then director of the Victoria and Albert Museum, Sir Roy Strong, defined it as a specialist museum of childhood with an extensive collection of toys and costumes.

Address Cambridge Heath Road, Bethnal Green E2 9PA | Getting there Underground to Bethnal Green (Central line); bus 8, 55, 254, 388 or 444 | Hours Daily 10am – 5.45pm | Tip This part of the East End is rather short of museums. However, a mile west is the elegant Geffrye furniture museum (136 Kingsland Road, Shoreditch), housed in a row of almshouses, which has a huge programme of activities for children.

62 — Old Chinatown

The last vestiges of pre-war East End Chinatown

Nowadays, hordes of people head to Soho to find London's Chinatown, but the capital's first Chinese area was in Limehouse, at the eastern end of the East End, where the first immigrants from the Far East settled in the late 18th century. They came in vessels that left the Orient and docked in east London. The Chinese crews were then left to fend for themselves. Often they jumped ship, choosing to starve on the streets of east London rather than return to the hell aboard. By the 1820s there were so many local down-and-out Chinese the government passed a law forcing the East India Company to provide basic essentials.

Some of those who settled in Limehouse opened grocery stores selling produce never previously seen in east London: areca nuts, betel leaves, lychees, dried seaweed and samshu, an alcoholic drink distilled from boiled rice or millet. Others went into gambling, which worried the authorities, but not as much as the opium dens did, captivating writers such as Oscar Wilde and Arthur Conan Doyle.

Charles Dickens set his last (unfinished) novel, *The Mystery of Edwin Drood* (1870), locally. At a Chinatown East End property Dickens found a Chinaman, a Lascar and a haggard woman 'blowing at a kind of pipe made of an old penny ink-bottle. The two first are in a sleep or stupor; the last is blowing at a kind of pipe, to kindle it.' In Wilde's *The Picture of Dorian Gray* (1890) the hero's party arrive at a 'small shabby house' where 'one could buy oblivion, the memory of old sins could be destroyed by the madness of sins.' Conan Doyle placed Holmes in disguise in such a den in one of his most remarkable short stories, *The Man with the Twisted Lip* (1891).

The authorities wiped out much of East End Chinatown with slum clearance in the 1930s, but somehow this small reminder has survived. The society runs a Chinese school and also a Chinese old people's club.

正義工商會

CHUN YEE SOCIETY
CHINESE SCHOOL ON SUNDAYS

CHUN YEE SOCIETY

工商會

50

Address Amoy Place, Canton Street and Ming Street area | Getting there Westferry LDR |
Hours Accessible 24 hours | Tip For the best evocation of old Chinatown, try the clichéd
but mesmerising early 20th-century novels of Thomas Burke and Sax Rohmer.

63 Olympic Bell

Immense silent bell created for the 2012 Olympics

The world's largest harmonically-tuned bell sits in Queen Elizabeth Park next to the Olympic London stadium, now home of West Ham United. The bell was created for the 2012 London Olympic Games. It is made of bronze, stands over 2 metres high, with a diameter of 3.3 metres, and weighs more than 22 tons. The bell is the second heaviest in Europe, after St Petersglocke in Cologne Cathedral. It is inscribed *Be not afeard. The isle is full of noises* from Caliban's speech in Shakespeare's *The Tempest*.

The (now sadly shut) Whitechapel Bell Foundry was supposed to construct the bell, but when their workings were found to have insufficient capacity it was sub-contracted to Royal Eijsbouts in Holland. Understandably there was some controversy about using a non-British firm.

The programme for the Olympic opening ceremony on Friday 27 July noted how 'bells ring out the changes of our days. They call us to wake, to pray, to work, to arms, to feast and, in times of crisis, to come together. Anyone born within hearing of the Bells of St Mary-le-Bow in Cheapside [in the City, not in the East End] has the right to call themselves "Cockney".'

The bell was rung at the start of the opening ceremony by Bradley Wiggins who had just won the Tour de France. Wiggins' action was symbolic; the hammer moved mechanically. Or as one journalist noted: 'He may be a superhuman athlete but even Bradley Wiggins isn't capable of setting the Olympic Bell's monumental half-ton clapper in motion by hand!' The bell was also rung just before Paul McCartney sang 'Hey Jude', the ex-Beatle blaming his faltering start on the bell's unexpectedly loud sound. Sadly, it now seems that because the bell is so loud it will probably never be rung again. Wags have suggested that if it is to be rung only sparingly, it should do so for significant local events, such as when West Ham win the Premiership.

Address Queen Elizabeth Olympic Park, Stratford E20 2ST | Getting there Underground (Central and Jubilee lines), DLR and Overground to Stratford | Hours Accessible 24 hours | Tip The Bow Bells pub a mile south does not refer to the bells within whose sound a cockney is born. Those bells are in the City of London, not the East End.

64 __ The Orchard
A forgotten corner of London

On any list of the most obscure locations in London, the Orchard must come high. Even for strange East End sites, it takes some beating.

Named after a long-vanished pub, the Orchard is a tiny outcrop of land where two East End borders meet, the River Lea and River Thames, the eastern and the southern, and the *flâneur* feels they are at the very edge of the world. Here, the River Lea is also known as Bow Creek. On the other side of the Lea is Canning Town, technically Essex until boundary changes, with the Orchard, being in the East End, traditionally in Middlesex. There is but one road in, Orchard Place, lined with evidence of its heavily industrial past in adverts for long defunct shipping companies and a collection of fascinating and beautifully illustrated history display boards. The road takes some finding off the eerily empty Lower Lea Crossing.

Another name for the locale is Trinity Buoy Wharf, as it is home to Trinity House, responsible for marine safety, which set up here as long ago as the mid-1700s. Trinity House still tests buoys and other marine equipment here. But the real surprise in the Orchard is London's only working lighthouse, dating from 1864 and built for research. Here, Michael Faraday, one of the leading scientists of the 19th century, pioneered the idea of an electric-powered lighthouse.

Until 1928 flooding, the Orchard was home to a small settlement of people who must have felt they were the town that London (and time) had forgotten. Slum clearance saw them off. Twenty years ago, the Orchard and Trinity Buoy Wharf was derelict. Now there are studios for people in the creative industries, and spaces for arts events. The Orchard's other features are an American-style diner, which looks as if it's the last restaurant on Earth, apartments made out of shipping containers, and Alunatime, London's first public Moon and Tide Clock.

Address Poplar E14 0JW | Getting there East India DLR | Hours Accessible 24 hours |
Tip Fascinating exploration is to be had just to the west searching for remnants of the
mostly filled-in East India Docks with a suitable OS map.

65 Peasants' Revolt Reminder

Where the king met the people

The White Hart pub, one of the few left locally, is built on the site of where the 14-year-old king, Richard II, rode out to Mile End in 1381 to negotiate with the leaders of the Peasants' Revolt.

The infamous revolt had started east of London on 30 May, 1381 when the king tried to levy a tax – a poll tax – on all the population to make up for the cost of his unsuccessful war against France. But the peasants were not just protesting against the government. There was general discontent following the Black Death epidemic of 1348. It had led to a shortage of workers. Wages rose but Parliament set a maximum wage. The radical priest, John Ball, enthused people, demanding that all men should be free and equal, and that wealth should be distributed more fairly. In a famous sermon he asked: 'When Adam delved and Eve span, who was then the gentleman?' As the peasants, led by Wat Tyler, streamed into London, the king took to the Tower for safety. This didn't stop the rebels entering the building, killing the Lord Chancellor and the Lord High Treasurer.

On 14 June, Richard met the rebels at Mile End and agreed to most of their demands. The next day the king met Tyler and the rebels at Smithfield in the City. Violence broke out, and Ralph de Standish, a servant of the king, killed Tyler as Sir John Newton, another servant, called him 'the greatest thief and robber in all Kent.' To defuse the situation, Richard promised to abolish serfdom. The peasants dispersed, but government men toured the villages hanging men who had taken part in the Revolt. Although the Revolt failed, its demands, for freedom, equality and money to the poor, were later accepted.

Richard II used as his symbol the white hart, a very rare beast, often associated in pageantry with Jesus Christ. The name of the beast fitted as a pun on his name Richard: rich heart/white hart.

Address The White Hart, 1 Mile End Road, Whitechapel E1 4TP | Getting there Underground (District and Hammersmith & City lines) and Overground to Whitechapel; bus 25, 205 or 254 | Hours Mon–Thu 11am–midnight, Fri 11–1am, Sat & Sun 9am–midnight | Tip A few yards to the east are the Trinity Green almshouses, built in 1695 to provide housing for '28 decay'd Masters & Commanders of Ships or ye Widows of such.' They were saved from demolition at the end of the 19th century and became the first buildings to be listed.

66 — The People's Palace
Elegant 1930s' version of a philanthropic dream

A glorious modernist structure, now part of Queen Mary's College, was built in 1886 as the East End's first cultural centre. The idea for something so ambitious in the East End was unique for those times. The catalyst was the novelist and social reformer Walter Besant who, in his 1882 work *All Sorts and Conditions of Men*, wrote the highly influential opener:

'Two millions of people, or thereabouts, live in the East End of London. They have no institutions of their own to speak of, no public buildings of any importance, no municipality, no gentry, no carriages, no soldiers, no picture-galleries, no theatres, no opera – they have nothing.'

Besant envisaged a 'Palace of Delight' as an alternative to drink and drudgery. The dream was realised and cost £75,000. It was to be a 'centre of intellectual and material advancement, recreation and amusement.' In 1887, the People's Palace opened. It was an instant success. More than 25,000 people visited it on a single Bank Holiday in 1888. One and a half million people visited in its first year. The library was run by women, open on Sunday and visited by about 1,000 people a day. Besant's friend, the mystery author Wilkie Collins, donated his own library.

Tragedy struck in February 1931 with a devastating fire. The hall was rebuilt in Portland Stone with reliefs by the country's top designer, Eric Gill. In 1934, the new People's Palace became part of Queen Mary's College. It was here that the local results of the 1945 General Election, which resulted in a Labour landslide, were declared. When the pictures were relayed around the world they showed the new prime minister, Clement Attlee, standing next to the Stepney victor, Phil Piratin, a Communist. The Americans, about to embark on the Cold War against the Soviets to vanquish communism, were horrified. It is now used for graduation ceremonies, lectures and special events.

Address Mile End Road, Bethnal Green E1 4NS | Getting there Underground to Stepney Green (District and Hammersmith & City lines); bus 25, 205 or 277 | Hours Mon–Fri 9am–6pm and also for special events; www.qmhospitality.co.uk or contact +44 (0)207 882 8175 | Tip At the back of the college is a small Jewish Sephardic – Spanish and Portuguese – cemetery where the gravestones are laid flat to symbolise how everybody is equal in death.

67 _ Petticoat Lane
Everything from fruit to fashion

Petticoat Lane is London's, nay Britain's, most famous market. Sometimes the crowds are so intense the passer-by or *flâneur* is drawn into buying for want of being able to move. However, many of the thousands perambulating its length will testify that it is not what it was.

Technically Petticoat Lane is Middlesex Street, the traditional boundary between the City of London and the East End. It first appeared in 1608 as a Spanish affair, later taken over by Huguenots (French Protestants). The market has always been dominated by clothes, which nowadays means anything from street-cred clubbing togs to fake designer goods via last year's Goth mufti. But there is still an unhealthy smattering of wonderfully useless bric-à-brac.

The dominance of clothing stems from textiles being one of the few professions open to immigrants in the past. All around were sweatshops where wage slaves toiled 13-hour days fixing, filling, button-holing and pressing, the foul atmosphere thick with woollen particles. The market also attracted the worst sort, such as thimble-riggers, card sharps and assorted swindlers. The food was better: thinly-cut cakes known as 'boolers' made of egg, flour and candied peel with a slight touch of saffron; Spanish olives; Dutch cucumbers; Norwegian herrings steeped in brine; German sausages; Scotch smoked salmon; and Polish chollas (long plaited loaves). The lingua franca was Yiddish, a Babylonian mix of German, Russian and Hebrew, well suited to the cut-throat atmosphere of the market and rich enough in dramatic-sounding heavily-guttural cusses to be particularly effective in warding off troublemakers.

When the Jews left the East End in the 1970s, the market was taken over by the new Bangladeshi immigrants, and the language and food changed appropriately. One stallholder no longer operating here is Alan (Lord) Sugar who cut his trading teeth on Sundays in the 1960s.

Address Middlesex Street, Spitalfields E1 7JF | **Getting there** Underground (Central, Circle and Hammersmith & City Lines) and National Rail to Liverpool Street | **Hours** Mon–Fri 8am–4pm, Sun 9am–2pm | **Tip** There are so many markets in the East End, the choice is overwhelming. But after a saunter down Petticoat Lane, head east for the world-renowned Brick Lane.

68 Plastic Factory

Shabby setting for a remarkable invention

After becoming the most exciting new substance of the 20th century, it is now the victim of a massive backlash. It is of course plastic and it was invented just outside the traditional East End in Hackney Wick. The once wonder material was the brainchild of Birmingham-born Alexander Parkes who wasn't even trained as a scientist or chemist. He simply mixed nitric and sulphuric acid with cotton, vegetable oils and organic solvents, pressing the dough into moulds to make new types of combs, pens, buttons and a thousand other things. He called it Parkesine. In 1862 he displayed it at Kensington's International Exhibition and was awarded a bronze medal. Parkes was also granted 66 patents for other ingenious developments. He patented a method for vulcanising rubber, which the engineer Thomas Hancock described as 'one of the most valuable and extraordinary discoveries of the age.' He electroplated works of art, one of which he presented to Prince Albert.

Parkes launched the Parkesine Company in 1866 with £100,000 but two years later went bust. In these early days of the substance his plastic just wasn't good enough. Complaints flooded in that his combs 'became so wrinkled and contorted as to be useless' within a few weeks. Maybe he was distracted, what with 17 children and 2 wives.

After Parkes went bust his manager, Daniel Spill, bought his patents and set up the Xylonite Company in 1869 in another Hackney Wick factory. There, Spill manufactured the first significant amounts of plastic commercially. Xylonite later became known in America as celluloid.

The Science Museum in Kensington holds more than 300 Parkesine objects in its collection, although most are too fragile to put on permanent show, the supposedly indestructible plastic withering away. The one thing Parkes didn't do though was to discover a means of ecologically disposing of the stuff.

Address Wallis Road, Hackney Wick E9 5NB | Getting there Overground to Hackney Wick; bus 276 | Hours Accessible 24 hours | Tip Travelling from Hackney Wick station to Bow in July 1864, Thomas Briggs of Clapton had the misfortune to become the first person in Britain to be murdered on a train. The murderer, Franz Müller, was apprehended at sea, fleeing to New York, and hanged in public outside Newgate Prison in the City of London.

69 — Politics Changed Here

Setting for the cataclysmic Limehouse Declaration

Inside this exquisite Georgian property, set on a lengthy street that hugs the Thames, one of the most significant events in modern British political history took place on 25 January, 1981. Four Labour Party politicians, the 'Gang of Four', issued their Limehouse Declaration, a savage attack on Labour's lurch left.

The Gang of Four comprised David Owen, ex-foreign secretary, who lived here; Roy Jenkins, who had been deputy prime minister; one-time transport minister Bill Rodgers; and the figure who many had thought would be the country's first woman prime minister, Shirley Williams. Owen's wife, Debbie, typed up their manifesto inside 78 Narrow Street and a colleague raced off to the Savoy Hotel to get it photocopied. When they returned, they found the media camped on the doorstep, having scoured their A–Z s to find this obscure East End location, the street a favourite of Dickens whose grandfather had lived nearby.

The Gang of Four soon formed a new organisation, the Social Democratic Party (SDP). Across the country, moderate Labour councillors and MPs flocked to the new party, causing the biggest upheaval in politics since a previous Labour Party split in 1931, while opponents howled accusations of treachery. The name the 'Gang of Four' fitted in neatly with the Limehouse setting for that was the name originally used to describe a group of recent Chinese dissidents, and Limehouse was home to London's first Chinese community in the 18th century.

Ironically, the SDP split the non-Tory vote at the 1983 General Election and solidified the premiership of the ultra-Conservative Margaret Thatcher. The SDP later merged with the Liberals to form the Liberal Democrats. Another irony was that their politics were adopted successfully at the polls a decade later by Tony Blair, whose 'New Labour' manifesto was modelled on that of the SDP.

Address 78 Narrow Street, Limehouse E14 8BP | **Getting there** Limehouse DLR | **Hours** Viewable from the outside only | **Tip** Narrow Street is one of the most sought-after in the East End as its exquisite Georgian properties and formidable converted warehouses hug a panoramic sweep of the Thames. Other notables who have lived here include the film director David Lean (*Great Expectations*, *Lawrence of Arabia*) and the irascible multi-million pound selling artist Francis Bacon.

70 Poplar Rates Mural
An extravagant display of political protest

Municipal warfare broke out in Poplar in 1921 when the Liberal Coalition government under David Lloyd George announced that all boroughs had to pay into a central fund to pay for services. Poverty-stricken Labour-run Poplar, led by the Christian pacifist George Lansbury, refused, asking why they, in one of the poorest areas in Britain, should be subsidising richer boroughs.

Under Lansbury, Poplar had become one of the first London councils to provide baths, washhouses and free libraries. It had introduced a minimum wage, and paid equal salaries to men and women. Local sanitation was better than in most similar areas and death rates were lower than in other parts of the East End. Nevertheless, the councillors were summoned to appear in court on 29 July, 1921 for non-payment. To show the world their plight, they marched from Poplar Town Hall to the High Court led by the official mace-bearer, a brass band and banner-waving supporters. Thirty councillors were found guilty of contempt of court and sent to jail; the men to Brixton, the women to Holloway. At Brixton, the men held council meetings in Lansbury's cell. When other councils expressed support for Poplar, the government relented. Success!

Lansbury was elected to Parliament for Bow and Bromley in 1910 but soon resigned his seat to win a fresh mandate on a 'Votes for Women' platform – and lost. In 1929 he returned to Parliament, became a minister, and in 1931 Labour leader by accident when the Labour prime minister, Ramsay MacDonald, formed a National Government with the Tories and Liberals. Eight years later, Lansbury travelled to Berlin to meet Hitler and Mussolini in a daring but fruitless attempt to seek peace. Ironically, his home, 39 Bow Road, was one of the first East End houses to be destroyed by German bombs.

The mural was painted as part of the protest against the Tories' late 1980s' poll tax.

Address Hale Street, Poplar E14 0BU | Getting there Poplar DLR; bus 15, 115 or D6 | Hours Accessible 24 hours | Tip At 117 Poplar High Street, an old town hall has been converted into the upmarket Lansbury Heritage Hotel, the only such establishment in the country named after a former leader of the Labour Party. The sale of the building was not without controversy, local councillors complaining about the knock-down price.

71 Prince of Streets
Home to centuries of immigrants

Princelet Street (previously Prince's Street) was at the centre of Jewish immigration into the East End in the late 19th century. Miriam Moses, social reformer and the first woman mayor of Stepney, was born at number 17 in 1886. In the 1960s there were new immigrants. In 1971, there were 200 Bengalis occupying just 16 addresses in Princelet Street. That soon changed. Gentrification of this little corner of Spitalfields has seen the properties stay out of reach of all but the super rich.

The social history is epitomised by number 19. This is different. In 1869, a synagogue was built in the garden, but when workmen began renovation in the 1980s they found a locked room that had been vacated in a hurry by the former caretaker, David Rodinsky. It was piled high with 78rpm discs, congealed food and a calendar for January 1963 marked in cuneiform and dotted with notes about the Hittite kings. It now houses a museum of immigration, mostly open by appointment, set up at the end of the 20th century by the Spitalfields Centre charity to create a permanent exhibition and educational resource.

Some other unusual legacies of the Jewish days remain. A relief of a viola on a coal hole on the pavement at the western end of the street honours the early 20th-century viola player Lionel Tertis who lived at number 8. At number 3 was the ill-fated Hebrew Dramatic Club, London's first Yiddish theatre, built by the local butcher. The venue was recalled by Israel Zangwill in his great East End novel *Children of the Ghetto* (1892): 'The only real theatre in London. The English stage – Drury Lane – pooh! It is not in harmony with the people: it does not express them.' A terrible tragedy occurred at the theatre on Tuesday 18 January, 1887 when someone cried 'Fire' in the middle of a performance of *The Gypsy Girl*. In the rush to leave, 17 people died in the crush.

Address Princelet Street, Spitalfields E1 6QH | Getting there Overground to
Shoreditch High Street | Hours By appointment. The Museum of Immigration and
Diversity organises occasional group open days; contact +44 (0)207 247 5352 or email
office@19princeletstreet.org.uk | Tip The remarkable story of the rediscovered room
is captured in the 1999 book *Rodinsky's Room* by Rachel Lichtenstein and the leading
contemporary East End writer, Iain Sinclair, which combines an oral history of Spitalfields with the quest to unravel the Rodinsky riddle.

72 Prison Cocktail Bar

Bar based on California's Alcatraz Prison

Only in Brick Lane, London's most exciting street, could there be a themed bar situated behind unassuming shutters based on a place nobody would ever want to go to – California's Alcatraz Prison. In this joint, inmates, sorry, revellers, *choose* to be convicted, and once inside, despite being on the right side of the law, enter an exciting world of mischief, smuggling in liquor to make bespoke cocktails forged by the mixologistical warders.

Alcohol has to remain hidden from the warden while inside; however, visitors are also encouraged to be as creative as they can while attempting to smuggle in liquor. Another way of looking at it is that the crooked guards are on your side and have a system for hiding contraband; just make sure the warden doesn't spot anything amiss.

As with all such units there is a regular routine. Once inside Alcotraz, revellers are met by Inmate no. 88. Felons are then expected to change into orange prison suits and sit inside the metallic cells to follow the legend of the Cassidys, a family of pirates, bootleggers and criminals. There is even shouting, or should that be shooting, interrogations, cell searches and a line-up as hipsters are punished for their love of a pop-up.

Alcotraz was founded by Sam Shearman who gave up his marketing job at Cadbury to pursue a passion for immersive events. He has explained how 'from entrance guests are transported into a world seen only in film and TV, with mind-blowing attention to every little detail.' How appropriate that the bar should be on Brick Lane, a street that has long been immersed in violence, though not these days fortunately, and was at the centre of the 1888 Jack the Ripper killings. Success for Alcotraz was instant, although lags keep reoffending – there were more than 3,000 tickets sold in one month – publicity even coming from San Francisco, home of the original Alcatraz.

Address 212 Brick Lane, Shoreditch E1 6SA, +44 (0)203 109 0488, www.alcotraz.co.uk |
Getting there Overground to Shoreditch High Street | Hours Tue 6–10.15pm (Master-
class), Wed & Thu 6.15–10.15pm, Fri 5–11.15pm, Sat 12.30–11.15pm, Sun 1.45–5.45pm |
Tip There are no real prisons anywhere near Brick Lane, but less than a mile east, on
Bethnal Green Road, is the old police station where George Orwell was once incarcerated.

73_The Ragged School Museum

Victorian values rule in a period museum

This Victorian-themed museum opened in 1990 in a group of canal-side buildings that once formed the largest ragged, or free, school in London, at one time run by the great charity pioneer, Dr Thomas Barnardo himself.

Ragged schools provided a free education in working-class districts for destitute children in the days before the 1870 Education Act brought millions into the compulsory system with a basic education for all children aged between 5 and 13. They took children who had been excluded from Sunday School because of their demeanour and behaviour. The emphasis was on reading, writing, arithmetic, and study of the Bible.

Thomas Barnardo came to the East End, instead of becoming a missionary in China, in 1866. He opened a school in Limehouse and one night, while locking up, spotted a dishevelled shoeless boy in the street. Barnardo couldn't believe the boy was homeless, and was then even more astonished to find there were hundreds and hundreds more. Six years later he opened a home for destitute children in Stepney and in 1877 the Copperfield Road Free School here, in what were originally warehouses for goods transported along the Regent's Canal that runs outside. The buildings were threatened with demolition in the 1980s but were saved by locals.

The museum is about more than just artefacts. Many of the visiting children come from schools in Tower Hamlets which, ironically, has one of the worst league table records in modern times. They meet actors dressed in period costume who take the children back in time, role-playing as strict Victorian teachers, revealing which period punishments are no longer socially acceptable. To some visitors' chagrin, the Victorian teachers can't impose endless detention or use the cane.

Address 46–50 Copperfield Road, Bow E3 4RR, +44 (0)208 980 6405, www.raggedschoolmuseum.org.uk | Getting there Underground to Mile End (Central, District and Hammersmith & City lines) | Hours Wed & Thu 10am–5pm, school lesson on first Sunday of each month 2–5pm | Tip In remarkable contrast with the horrors of slum Victorian East End captured at the museum is the welcome local green lung, Mile End Park, a lengthy longitudinal stretch between the Regent's Canal and Burdett Road, which ingeniously stretches over busy Mile End Road.

74 Richard Green Statue

Superstar sailor with statue and one-eared dog

Richard Green (1803–63), shipowner and philanthropist, was one of the greatest seamen to come out of the East End. Born locally at Blackwall in 1803, he joined the family firm as a shipwright and learned his craft fitting out whalers. The firm, which became known as Green, Wigram and Green, took advantage of the East India Company's charter to build the renowned East Indiamen vessels.

In 1833, the company launched the *Monarch*, then the largest steamship ever built in the country. It was even powered by two 100 hp engines designed by Britain's greatest engineers, Matthew Boulton and James Watt. Green and Co. struck gold in Australia, and capitalised on the goldrush, but Richard Green was no mere speculator. Guided by his motto, that 'he had no time to hesitate', he expended considerable energy promoting maritime welfare. He spent time improving the men's conditions, built a hospital, established a sailors' home, donated to the orphans' asylum, organised instruction courses for navigators, and supported schools in Poplar in days long before universal education. His death in 1863 was noted in the *Illustrated London News* as 'little less than a calamity.' In his will, Green left huge sums to a large number of charitable bequests, including a free gift of the building and a perpetual endowment for his Sailors' Home in Poplar.

Green's statue stands outside Poplar Baths. The face was taken from his death mask. He is accompanied by his dog Hector who sadly lost its ear in 1967 when a boy got stuck climbing the statue to retrieve his swimming trunks. The Fire Brigade arrived and realised that the only way to cut the boy away was to chip off the ear. On the side of the statue there are reliefs commemorating Green's shipbuilding exploits, including one of the record-breaking clipper *Challenger*, which he built in 1852 to challenge American rivals in the tea trade.

HENRY PRINCE & COMPY
Statue Foundry Southwark

RICHARD CREE

Address 170 East India Dock Road, Poplar E14 0EH | Getting there All Saints DLR |
Hours Accessible 24 hours | Tip A few hundred yards to the west, in Poplar Park, is a sad
memorial to 18 children aged 5 years old killed not in World War II but in World War I,
in 1917, by a bomb dropped from a Gotha aircraft in a daylight raid on a nearby school.

75 _ River Police
The oldest local police force in the world

The sight of police boats bobbing up and down by the Wapping shore never fails to mesmerise those exploring the river. Who knows, at any moment a call might come in and the peelers in their mountainous waterproofs will be scrambling into a motor boat, hot in pursuit of a gnarled villain who has just exited the Tower of London deviously escaping on a skiff armed with the Crown Jewels.

The river police, based in Wapping, is the oldest localised police force in the world. It was founded in 1798 to coincide with the creation of the many London docks. At that time, crime was escalating as more and more ships came in laden with luxury goods following the opening up of the Americas and the Far East. As security improved, so did looting. Those East Indiamen and clippers stuffed with whisky, rum and ivory were just too much of a temptation. Empty vessels left unguarded could be stripped of everything that could be easily removed – and the fixtures, even the rigging. There were many types of waterborne felons, and all with exotic names: night plunderers, light-horsemen, heavy-horsemen, scufe-hunters and rat catchers.

The creation of a river police was not greeted amicably by all East Enders. A mob of 2,000 attempted to burn down the original police office – with the police inside. Even among the establishment there was opposition. The idea of a salaried police was considered an affront to the ruling class, who preferred *ad hoc* justice at a time when law and order could be profitable for both sides.

It was not only crime that occupied the river police's time. In September 1878, the worst maritime disaster in Thames history occurred when the *Princess Alice* pleasure steamer collided with a coal boat and sank. More than 700 people drowned. The disaster was exacerbated by the number of pickpockets who appeared, as well as looters who wanted to pick at the wreckage.

Address 98 Wapping High Street, Wapping E1W 2NE | Getting there Overground to Wapping | Hours Accessible 24 hours | Tip The Thames River Police Museum, which is located in what was once the carpenter's workshop at the police station, is an excellent way to discover the full story of the water bobbies. Visits are by prior arrangement only – contact curator@thamespolicemuseum.org.uk

76 River Thames' Best View

Stunning and surprising view of London river

A small gap in the buildings at the eastern end of Limehouse's Narrow Street offers the *flâneur* the most mesmerising view of the Thames to be found in London. Here, at an appropriate bend, the river is at its very widest. To the west is a long stretch of oily brown water leading towards Shadwell, the Tower and Central London, the supreme sight of the Shard prominent in the distance. To the south, the river washes the west side of the long Isle of Dogs alongside Canary Wharf.

Stand here to soak in centuries of history, to imagine the thousands of explorers, warriors, colonialists, pirates, privateers who have sailed past here on their way to open up, or attack, or exploit, or emigrate to the ends of the Earth. Martin Frobisher's 16th-century flotilla heading out to the Atlantic to find the North-West Passage, a supposed quick route north of Canada to China. Thousands of Jews arriving from East Europe in the late 19th century, convinced (for a few hours) that they had arrived in New York. An 18th-century Thames with boats from far-off lands filled with German stevedores in light-blue jackets and yellow trousers, or Scandinavians smelling of tallow and turpentine, or tigerish-looking Malays smoking foot-long cheroots, or Yugambeh people from the Gold Coast arrayed in necklaces of charms and fetishes, or Neapolitans wearing images of their guardian saint.

This part of the Thames has been mesmerising, menacing and worrying to many writers. In Charles Dickens' last full novel, the equally mesmerising *Our Mutual Friend* (1865), Lizzie and Gaffer Hexam make a living trawling the East End sections for victims of drowning, emptying their pockets before they pass the corpse on to the police. To Joseph Conrad it was 'one of the dark places on the Earth,' where his characters on a vessel begin to relate the nightmare journey into the *Heart of Darkness* in the 1899 novel of the same name.

Address Narrow Street, Limehouse E14 8DQ | Getting there Limehouse DLR and National Rail | Hours Accessible 24 hours | Tip So much water around here! Snazzy Limehouse Basin Marina is easily accessible off Narrow Street. At its northern end, it provides the terminus to the Regent's Canal, part of the national canal network. To the north-east is the Limehouse Cut that leads to the River Lea.

77 Roa – Street Artist
Celebrating urban wildlife

Roa is no mere street artist. People come from all over to admire his handiwork, fittingly splashed across the shabbiest parts of the old East End. He comes from Ghent in Belgium and is almost as enigmatic as Banksy. His anonymity has kept his work and his spirit free, but the popularity of street art caught up with him by 2009. He started to receive invitations and commissions, including permission in the East End to paint the side of buildings.

Roa uses a spray can and painting rolls. His renown rests on a penchant for giant beasts, brutes and black-and-white animal street art. Roa started painting animals on abandoned buildings and warehouses in isolated industrial areas back home. He soon spread to Warsaw, Paris, New York and the East End.

Dedicated to animal welfare and wildlife preservation, Roa's most famous creation is a heron on Hanbury Street, just off Brick Lane. It is painted over five storeys, its mass typical of his regular style, some of the biggest paintings in the history of street art. While he was working on it, a Bengali man commented 'you're painting a crane, a bird sacred to our culture.' So the locals now refer to it as a crane.

The politics of street art has changed. In the 20th century, all street art was considered to be illegal. After Roa created a 12-foot rabbit, Hackney council threatened to paint it over. This is the same body who painted over a Banksy in 2009 after letting it stand for eight years. There was an outcry and so the council reversed its stance. Nowadays it is all done with permission. A Liverpool pub was recently sold with a mural on one wall advertised hopefully as a Banksy with a pub attached, thereby doubling its value. Artists now use the street to publicise exhibitions. Mobster, a stenciller from Newcastle, mocked this with a street mural here in Spitalfields declaring: *This Will be Available on Canvas Later.*

Address Hanbury Street, Spitalfields E1 6QR | Getting there Underground to Liverpool Street (Circle, Central and Hammersmith & City lines) and National Rail | Hours Accessible 24 hours | Tip Here at the old Truman brewery are a pair of abandoned cars. The upper one is a 2008 piece by D*Face. The lower was decorated by Banksy around the same time. It is protected by a Perspex box.

78_Robin Hood Gardens

Nightmarish brutalist concrete council estate

Seeing is believing at the East End's most notorious, most vilified council estate. Robin Hood Gardens is the ultimate in austere, frightening, brutalist concrete hideousness, described by critics as the worst peace-time housing disaster in London's history.

The estate was the brainchild of Peter and Alison Smithson. Their mid-1960s' Economist building in St James' should have been enough to warn people what might happen if they were let loose on a housing scheme. The land was first developed in the 19th century. Back-to-back houses were built, but soon became slums. In 1885, seven tenement blocks replaced them and were demolished in 1965.

The Smithsons' thinking was that the tightly packed brick houses of the old East End could be reformatted into 'streets in the sky'. They created two long curved blocks of elevated concrete facing each other across a central green space – which of course were absolutely nothing like the old houses. Residents now felt cut off, unable to cope with the inevitable outbreaks of anti-social behaviour. To make matters worse, the site was hemmed in by the thunderous sounds of the Blackwall Tunnel Approach.

Peter Smithson later admitted that the project had failed. 'In other places you see doors painted and pot plants outside houses, the minor arts of occupation, which keep the place alive. In Robin Hood, if someone were to put anything out people will break it.' The response was that if you put people in what Tower Hamlets councillors likened to a particularly nasty East German Stalinist concentration camp, they might not behave as genteelly as if they were living by the sea in Lyme Regis.

To the residents, its demise can't come quickly enough. Yet there are architecture writers who with a straight face laud its concrete mass as a breakthrough in municipal housing. Part of a now-demolished section of the building has been preserved by the V&A Museum.

Address Robin Hood Gardens, 129 Woolmore Street, Poplar E14 0HG | Getting there Blackwall DLR | Hours Accessible 24 hours | Tip Half a mile to the north is the more respected and attractive 26-storey Balfron Tower, designed in 1963 by the leading modernist Ernö Goldfinger in a similar vein to his lauded Trellick Tower.

79 Roman Wall
They came, they saw, they built walls

Just outside Tower Hill tube station, 10.6 metres high, stands one of the most formidable extant sections of London's ancient stone walls. The upper sections date back to the 12th and 17th centuries, but the oldest sections were started around the year 200 by the Roman conquerors to protect Londinium.

The Romans arrived in London in 43 AD. They weren't invited. They invaded. They stayed for around 400 years and departed in the year 410 AD. To build these walls they quarried around one million blocks of Kent ragstone and brought it here in some 1,750 boatloads along the Thames. The mortar for the wall was mixed with olive oil and fats to help make it waterproof and prevent frost forming. Roman walls began to decay in Saxon times, but the Normans rebuilt and heightened large sections, adding numerous gates that separated the city from the suburbs. The major gates into the East End included Aldgate and Bishopsgate, long gone, but remembered in street names.

The Roman walls gradually began to disappear as locals removed blocks for their own properties. But preservation followed after the *Illustrated London News* of Saturday 24 June, 1843 made Londoners realise the importance of the few remaining stretches: 'Our illustration shows the only considerable portion of the old City Wall which now remains; it is behind the houses in Trinity-square, Tower-hill. It was given up by the Corporation, some few years since, to be pulled down; but the relic has been respited to the present day; and now has arisen a fresh anxiety as to its preservation.'

In 1852, a workman, having his lunch, absent-mindedly kicked a block of stone and uncovered a substantial Roman stone tomb, part of the burial place of Gaius Julius Alpinus Classicianus, Procurator of Roman Britain 61 – 65 AD in the wake of Boadicea's revolt. A replica has been placed in the modern wall alongside the old City Wall.

Address By Tower Hill tube station, EC3N 4DJ | Getting there Underground to Tower Hill (Circle and District lines) | Hours Accessible 24 hours | Tip Following the trace of the wall around this part of London is not as easy, as most of it has long been destroyed. Near the station on Cooper's Row is a hotel, in the courtyard of which the wall has been preserved, the hotel having been built around it. Other sections still stand in the old City.

80 Rough Trade East

Legendary record store – never out of fashion

Record shops mostly don't exist any more. They seem to have gone the way of blacksmiths and seed merchants. But Rough Trade survives and thrives. It has become an institution with shops in New York, Nottingham, Notting Hill, Bristol and most recently in the revitalised old Ben Truman brewery off Brick Lane.

Mild-mannered Geoff Travis began Rough Trade on Portobello Road market in the mid-1970s but then moved into a former head shop on Kensington Park Road, right in the middle of hip, hippy Ladbroke Grove. It was the perfect time. Punk exploded across the capital in 1977 and Rough Trade became an unofficial HQ to rival Malcolm McLaren and Vivienne Westwood's Sex boutique on King's Road. Bands hung out here, fans came in to lig, record company executives dropped in with the latest release, occasionally people bought records. Geoff Travis' ambition to run a London version of San Francisco's City Lights was working.

Rough Trade also successfully capitalised on the phase for independent record labels that swept the country in the late 1970s. The label initially released avant-garde groups that were never going to elicit mass appeal, but they also cleverly signed the leading purveyors of the new electronic sounds, Cabaret Voltaire, and in 1983 added the most exciting new group on the planet, The Smiths.

The retail side now acts independently from the label, but despite the failure of a branch in Neal's Yard, Covent Garden, Rough Trade prospers. Every item, whether vinyl or CD, contains descriptions to encourage browsing and discovery. As store director Stephen Godfroy has explained: 'You've got to create an environment where people want to spend time. It's got to be distinctive, have confidence in recommending exciting new products, and not rely on chart product.' As well as selling records in all sorts of formats, Rough Trade East also hosts successful gigs.

Address Old Truman Brewery, 91 Brick Lane, Spitalfields E1 6QL, +44 (0) 0207 392 7788,
www.roughtrade.com | Getting there Overground to Shoreditch High Street | Hours
Mon–Thu 9am–9pm, Fri 9am–8pm, Sat 10am–8pm, Sun 11am–7pm | Tip Head down
Brick Lane to its Aldgate East continuation, tiny Osborne Street. There, in an old Victorian
warehouse, at nos. 9–13, is the former Sarm East studio where 'Bohemian Rhapsody'
was mixed and early versions of the Clash's exciting 'White Man in Hammersmith Palais'
were rehearsed.

81 The Royal Mint

Handsome former home of the money supply

The Royal Mint, the body that produces the country's money supply, occupied this spot from 1809 to 1967. In mediaeval times this was the setting for the mediaeval Cistercian Abbey of Eastminster, the East End's version of the somewhat better known Westminster. The abbey buildings were taken down when the Mint moved here from the nearby Tower of London. To herald the move, the keys from the old mint were ceremoniously delivered to the Constable of the Tower. New buildings, such as Johnson and Smirke's surviving handsome Georgian façade building, went up here for staff such as the Assay Master and the Provost of the Moneyers. The entire site was protected by a boundary wall patrolled by the Royal Mint's military guard.

The Mint wasn't working efficiently by the 1850s. There were irregularities in the quality and weight of the coinage. The Prime Minister, Lord Palmerston, threatened a break-up. However, a German chemist, George Ansell, saved the day, improving the weighing system, replacing the old scales and tightening up on the amount of gold that was being lost. Help came from the Rothschild banking family who secured a lease from the government in 1852 to set up the Royal Mint Refinery at nearby 19 Royal Mint Street.

When the Great War broke out in 1914, the Chancellor, David Lloyd George, removed gold coins from circulation to help pay for the war effort, replacing them with less-romantic paper money. During World War II, work moved away from the East End and the bombs to Pinewood film studios in Buckinghamshire. There, the Mint ensured people were paid with coins, rather than paper money. This was to counteract the Nazis' fiendish plan of flooding the country with forged notes. More upheaval loomed in 1966 following the government's decision to decimalise the currency, and the Mint moved to Wales. The buildings are now owned by the Chinese government.

Address Royal Mint Court, Whitechapel EC3N 4QN | Getting there Underground to Tower Hill (Circle and District lines); Tower Gateway DLR; bus 42, 78, 100 or 343 | Hours Viewable from the outside only | Tip Given the existence of Westminster, there had to be an Eastminster. The monastery stood where the Mint was later built but was dissolved in 1538. Large-scale excavation of the site took place in the 1980s. The results can be seen in the Museum of London.

82 Sad Shadwell

The forgotten hamlet, full of unusual engineering

Lost between weird Wapping and stolid Stepney, Shadwell was all but obliterated by world war bombing and 1960s' slum clearance. But some exciting major features remain: mostly abandoned Tobacco Dock, the massive, eerie, lonely Shadwell Basin, just off the Thames, and its spectacular bascule bridge.

In the 13th century the area was a low-lying marsh, Scadflet or Shatfliet. A church was dedicated to St Chad, and alongside a well. In Roman times there was a port, but by the 16th century the hamlet had mostly been abandoned. Change came with the expansion of the docks early in the 19th century. Shadwell Basin was built between 1828 and 1832. Further expansion took place once it was realised that the entrance was too small to accommodate the new larger ships. The area became rough and ready. Journalist William Blanchard Jerrold wrote of 'the densely packed haunts of poverty and crime – in the hideous tenements stacked far and wide, round such institutions as the Bluegate Fields ragged schools in Shadwell.'

By the start of the 20th century the docks in this part of the East End had become outdated. Cargoes were being unloaded downriver and then taken by barge to warehouses here. It was uneconomic. These docks were the first to close – in 1969. Fortunately, the basin was not filled in. The London Docklands Development Corporation, one of the most successful quangos in London history, began a programme of redevelopment, building apartment blocks around what is one of the most surprising stretches of water away from the Thames, now used for sailing, canoeing and fishing. Film lovers will spot its use as an exciting location shot in the 1946 Ealing classic *Hue and Cry*. At the eastern end of the basin is the unforgettable bascule bridge. Okay, it no longer bascules – it would tip up 45 degrees to allow vessels through – but every sight of this engineering masterpiece thrills.

Address Glamis Road, Shadwell E1W 3ED | Getting there Overground to Shadwell and DLR | Hours Accessible 24 hours | Tip To the north is the oddity of Tobacco Dock where the warehouses were redeveloped in the 1990s as a shopping centre – the 'Covent Garden of the East End', no less – that turned out to be an embarrassing failure. Exploring its recesses and corners is fascinating but frustrating.

83 Salvation à la Mode

William Booth brought redemption to the East End

The Salvation Army is one of the East End's greatest creations. A popular charity with a quasi-military structure, it was founded in 1865 by William Booth, a tall white-faced, dark-eyed, fierce-looking revivalist preacher who wore a great black beard over his chest. His statue stands here in Mile End. When he moved to London in 1849 he drew up a personal code of conduct that included such entreaties as 'I do promise – my God helping – that I will rise every morning sufficiently early. That I will as much as possible avoid all that babbling and idle talking in which I have lately so sinfully indulged.'

One evening in June 1865 he told missionaries at an open-air meeting outside the Blind Beggar pub that 'there is heaven in East London for everyone who will stop to think and look to Christ as a personal saviour.' Booth set up a mission that soon attracted many converts in a territory full of 'blaspheming infidels and boisterous drunkards.' He would come home 'night after night haggard with fatigue, his clothes torn and bloody, bandages swathing his head where a stone had struck,' his wife explained.

In 1878, he reorganised his mission along quasi-military lines as the Salvation Army, complete with army-styled ranks, Booth himself as the General. Their banner emblazoned in red, blue and gold sported a sun symbol and the motto 'Blood and Fire'. Soon the bands of the Salvation Army were marching into town 'to do Battle with the Devil and his Hosts.' Booth and Co. had no difficulty finding the diabolical in Whitechapel, comparing them to 'the Negroes in the Equatorial Forest. Their lot is not, perhaps, a very happy one, but is it so very much worse than that of many a pretty orphan girl in our Christian capital?' By the time Booth died, the Salvation Army had spread to 58 countries. It can now be found in more than 130 countries running charity shops and homeless shelters.

Address Outside 31 Mile End Road, Stepney E1 4TP | **Getting there** Underground (District and Hammersmith & City lines) and Overground to Whitechapel; bus 25 or 205 | **Hours** Accessible 24 hours | **Tip** Alongside William Booth's statue is that of his wife, Catherine, co-founder of the organisation and known as the 'Mother of the Salvation Army'.

84 Secret Burial Grounds

Cemeteries' link to a lost Jewish population

On the north side of busy Mile End Road, hidden within the Queen Mary University of London Campus, is the Novo Beth Chaim, a long-disused Jewish cemetery from 1733. It is the oldest entity in the area, given that almost everything else in Mile End, even the nearby canal, dates back no further than Victorian times.

Notables buried here include Benjamin D'Israeli (grandfather to the Prime Minister of similar name) and Daniel Mendonza, the prize-fighter of the 1830s. The gravestones are all flattened, a custom adopted by Sephardi – Mediterranean-area Jews – symbolising that everyone is equal in the sight of the Lord, so that no one should have a higher stone than anyone else. A large chunk of the plot was sold to the college by the Spanish and Portuguese Jews' Congregation in the 1970s. Thousands of graves were exhumed and reinterred in a site in Essex.

Harder to find, just to the west, behind Albert Stern House at 245 Mile End Road, is the Velho (Old) Cemetery. It was opened in 1657, when all this was countryside, just after Oliver Cromwell officially allowed Jews back into the country, and so is the oldest Jewish cemetery in the country. Those buried here include Simon de Caceres (d. 1704) who advised Cromwell on the defence of Jamaica. The cemetery closed in 1737. A Jewish hospital and old people's home stood alongside from 1790 to 1977.

Another rewarding find is the now closed Alderney Road Cemetery from 1697, hidden away behind brick walls. Alderney Road is Ashkenazi, for North European Jews. For decades it was a place of pilgrimage for both Jews and gentiles honouring the Kabbalah leader Chaim Jacob Samuel Falk (d. 1782). Falk had fled Germany, where he had been sentenced to death for sorcery, and in the capital became known as the 'Ba'al Shem' of London, a master of the secret names of God, with which He created the world, according to Hebrew mysticism.

Address West of Westfield Way, Mile End E1 4NS | **Getting there** Underground to Mile End (Central and Hammersmith & City lines); bus 25 or 205 | **Hours** Accessible 24 hours | **Tip** A pleasant afternoon can be spent searching round this little part of Mile End for signs of the vanished Jewish community.

85 Spice Island
Reminders of an exotic trade

For hundreds of years, British ships brought vast quantities of spice from the Far East into London. The ships unloaded at the East India Import Dock, a section of which survives, while all around are streets named after spices – clove, coriander, nutmeg, oregano, saffron and sorrel – built over the rest of the filled-in dock.

In charge was the East India Company that, by the early 19th century, was the most powerful commercial concern in the world. The company had been formed 200 years earlier by East End merchants who convinced Queen Elizabeth to allow them to exploit the huge Indian market on behalf of the Crown. Their vessels were kitted out as warships for protection against pirates and the rival Dutch. In 1609 they struck gold, or rather nutmeg, when Nathaniel Courthope led an expedition to the tiny East Indies island of Poolaroone, near Sumatra (now called Pulau Run).

Nutmeg could be used in soaps and perfume, and so it enjoyed a vastly inflated value. To buy the spice, the ship's company had to decide which British commodity the islanders would crave. In Britain, the main export at this time was woollen textiles. The natives didn't want the Harris Tweed cloth the sailors brought but they did take hard cash, a ha'penny securing 10 pounds of nutmeg in weight. Later expeditions saw the British bring fancy goods such as mirrors and ivory.

Courthope's team returned to London and sold the nutmeg at a tidy profit margin of 32,000 per cent. King James was so thrilled he styled himself king of England, Scotland, Ireland … and Poolaroone. The Dutch later murdered Courthope and took Poolaroone. In exchange, the English obtained the Dutch colony of New Amsterdam, that subsequently became Manhattan. The East India Company later endured an ignominious end. The government abolished its monopoly following the 1858 Indian Mutiny and it collapsed.

Address The streets south of East India Dock Road, east of A102, Poplar E14 2AA | Getting there East India DLR | Hours Accessible 24 hours | Tip Follow the roar west to the original Blackwall Tunnel (the more westerly of the two), considered a wonder of the age and a major engineering feat when it opened in 1897. The tunnel, linking Poplar and Charlton, was deliberately built with strange twists and kinks so that the horses could not see the chink of light in the distance and bolt.

86 Spitalfields Market

Bustling ancient market

This part of the East End is world famous for its markets (Petticoat Lane, Brick Lane) and Spitalfields is the oldest, 350 years strong. Local shock artists Gilbert and George once described Spitalfields Market as the most representative place on Earth. It is still bustling, despite endless corporate plans to sanitise and even kill it.

There has been a market here since 1638 when Charles I bestowed a licence for 'flesh, fowl and roots to be sold on Spittle Fields' – the fields by the 1197-built hospital and priory of St Mary's Spittle, demolished after the dissolution of the monasteries in 1539. The rights were strengthened by Charles II in 1682 when he granted John Balch a Royal Charter allowing him to hold a market every Thursday and Saturday in Spital Square.

Spitalfields itself has long attracted immigrants: Huguenots and the Irish at first, followed by Jews. At the end of the 20th century, Bangladeshi immigration changed the demography, but the market carried on. When the City of London Corporation acquired the market in 1920, new buildings went up, the adjacent Fruit & Wool Exchange became a rather crowded World War II shelter, and in 1991 the fruit and vegetable section moved to Leyton as New Spitalfields Market. But the old market survives. It majors in interesting clothes, bric-à-brac, mostly food, which fits in with its historical role, but sadly no longer books. By 2019 there were 44 retailers and restaurants, 88 market stalls and 25 street food traders under one Victorian Market Roof.

The surrounding area has long been a prime target for the most rapacious developers. After all, it is located right next to the City of London and the gigantic, glaring, granite skyscrapers of Bishopsgate. This century, much-loved buildings and spaces have been cleared away and Starbucked, leaving the few older structures even more conspicuous and incongruous.

Address 16 Commercial Street, Spitalfields E1 6EW | **Getting there** Underground (Circle, Central and Hammersmith & City lines) and National Rail to Liverpool Street; bus 8, 26, 35, 48, 78, 135, 149, 205 or 242 | **Hours** Mon–Fri 10am–8pm, Sat 10am–6pm, Sun 10am–5pm | **Tip** Old Spitalfields turns up at unlikely spots nearby. Head for Spital Square to the north-west of the market where at no. 37, in the elegant Georgian splendour of a silk merchant's house, resides the head office of the charity the Society for the Protection of Ancient Buildings (SPAB). Nearby is the even more obscure Spital Yard where there is a period plaque for the birthplace of Susanna Wesley, mother of John.

87 St Anne's Weather Vane

Symbols and signs rife at the old sailors' church

At the top of this early 18th-century Nicholas Hawksmoor church is a flagpole surmounted by a golden ball and a weather vane that features the four points of the compass. Below the ball a White Ensign flies. Until this century, Trinity House, dedicated to safeguarding shipping and seafarers, used it as a sea mark for navigating the Thames.

St Anne's, consecrated in 1730, was built in the Baroque style and shaped like a Greek Cross. It was one of 12 Queen Anne churches built after a 1711 Act of Parliament to accommodate London's expanded population. To raise the money, Parliament imposed a tax on coal coming up the River Thames. It has the second highest Gothic tower in Britain, beaten only by the Clock Tower of the Houses of Parliament. The pipe organ won first prize in the Great Exhibition of 1851 and is much prized by musicians. The clock, the first in the country to be illuminated, was set by checking with the visible observatory in Greenwich on the south bank. It used to chime four times every hour for the benefit of ships on the Thames.

The church graveyard features a major mystery: a large four-sided pyramid from 1730 built out of Portland stone. The top of one of the faces is inscribed with the words *The Wisdom of Solomon* and underneath a carved coat of arms with a unicorn. Beneath the English inscription are the same words in Hebrew. The pyramid's existence has baffled historians. Was it originally intended to be put on top of one of the towers? It simply fits in with architect Hawksmoor's obsession with Freemasonry and sacred geometry, numbers featured in the Bible and ancient texts giving instructions on which measurements and features to use in creating cities and erecting buildings to give them divine protection. Hawksmoor's churches and those of his mentor, Christopher Wren, contain many such signs and symbols.

Address 5 Newell Street, Limehouse E14 7HP | Getting there Westferry DLR; bus 15, 115, 135 or D3 | Hours Sundays, but intermittent other days | Tip Nicholas Hawksmoor's small collection of Baroque early 18th-century churches have become cult classics in recent years. St George-in-the-East, a mile and a half to the west, was badly damaged in World War II, but Christ Church Spitalfields attracts thousands of visitors a week.

88_ St George's Churchyard and Mortuary

Shattered church with a dramatic history

Nicholas Hawksmoor's churches are the greatest in the East End, although here the churchyard is now more interesting than the church, as much of the building was destroyed during the Blitz.

The church was built in 1729 when the local population was small but growing. In the 18th century, before the area became a slum, there was still a local bohemian community, epitomised by the area's most lauded resident, the Swedish visionary and mystic Emanuel Swedenborg. The horrors of the 1811 Ratcliffe Highway Murders were felt particularly hard here, the setting for the funerals of many of the victims.

The church was the setting in 1859 and 1860 for 18 months' worth of 'no Popery' riots. These broke out when parishioners discovered that the vicar, Bryan King, had established a secret Catholic brotherhood for priests known as the Society of the Holy Cross. So angry were some worshippers that during services they pelted the altar with bread and butter, and orange peel, brought in barking dogs, and spat on and kicked the clergy. They even urinated on the pews. Once the trouble had abated there were often as many as 50 police officers in the wings ready for trouble.

Of considerable interest in the grounds is a mysterious-looking mortuary, built in 1876, by which time the scourge of body-snatching had died down. Here the body of Jack the Ripper's third victim. Elizabeth Stride, was brought in 1888. The mortuary became a nature study museum in 1904, the smallest museum in London, but closed during World War II, never to reopen. The churchyard was featured in one of the greatest London films, *The Long Good Friday* (1980), as where gangster Harold Shand played by Bob Hoskins has his Rolls-Royce blown up. The original walls remain and within is the modern church.

Address 14 Cannon Street Road, St George's E1 0BH | Getting there Overground to Shadwell | Hours Sundays, but intermittent other days | Tip A quarter of a mile to the west, in Swedenborg Gardens, are some makeshift memorials to one of the greatest of Swedes. Emanuel Swedenborg was the first scientist to discover the pituitary gland before his epiphany caused him to become one of the leading theologians of the 18th century.

89 St Katharine Docks

Vibrant revamped marina next to the Tower

Two sculpted elephants guard one of the entrances to this magnificently restored dock by the Tower of London, where huge loads of ivory used to be unloaded from African ships, now filled with bars, restaurants, shops and yachts.

St Katharine Dock was designed by Thomas Telford, who also reworked London Bridge, and built between 1824 and 1828 on the site of the Royal Foundation of St Katharine charitable institution. The charity's church, St Katharine's, was pulled down to make room for the dock, as were the homes of more than 10,000 inhabitants. The soil excavated was shipped upstream to provide foundations for the new suburbs of Pimlico and Belgravia.

At St Katharine's the warehouses were built right up to the water so as to aid unloading and deter thieves from the valuable cargo: perfumes, wine, marble, spices and ivory. The docks used the latest technology: steam engines designed by James Watt and Matthew Boulton to keep the water level in the basins above that of the tidal river. Just before the start of the Great War in 1914, a German ship crammed with nationals set off to jeers from the locals. During World War II, St Katharine Dock was bombed and the warehouses around the eastern basin destroyed.

St Katharine Docks closed in 1968. Fortunately, they were *not* filled in and so could be expertly renovated. The Italianate Ivory House of 1854 has survived, as has the late 18th-century warehouse that is now the Dickens Inn, one of the largest pubs in London. New developments include the epic Tower Hotel, featured in 1980 East End gangster film *The Long Good Friday* and in many episodes of *The Bill*. Property magnate Nick Leslau bought the site in 2011 for £156 million and sold it in 2014 to the Blackstone Group for nearly £450 million. Residents in recent years have included the colourful Conservative politician David Mellor and the actor David Suchet.

Address East Smithfield, Tower Liberty, E1W 1LA | **Getting there** Underground to Tower Hill (Circle and District lines); Tower Gateway DLR | **Hours** Accessible 24 hours | **Tip** Head east to London Docks to see how *not* to redevelop a watery site. Bad decisions saw the docks east of Thomas More Street mostly filled in. The controversial fortress Wapping printing works for Rupert Murdoch's News International papers was built over the northern half of the filled-in Western Dock. There are new apartments alongside the small stretch of remaining water but the area has none of the vitality of St Katharine's or Canary Wharf.

90 Suffragette Centre

When the East End led the fight for women to vote

Bromley Public Hall, now Tower Hamlets Register Office, was a regular meeting place for Suffragettes in the early 20th century. The Suffragettes, led by the redoubtable and indefatigable Sylvia Pankhurst, took over much of Bow and Bromley-by-Bow in the years leading up to the Great War. Frustrated at the lack of success in her campaign to get women the vote in her native Manchester, the daughter of Emmeline Pankhurst moved to this grim slice of working-class London.

Sylvia's first act was to rent a bakery (since demolished) and paint 'VOTES FOR WOMEN' on the fascia. People threw fish-heads and bits of rolled-up newspaper soaked in urine at her. It didn't put her off. Next up: direct action. The Suffragettes organised a meeting for Valentine's Day 1913. When it ended, supporters marched to the local bank and police station, and smashed the windows. They wanted publicity in the papers. Sylvia Pankhurst and her American assistant, Zelie Emerson, were arrested. They quickly paid their fines. Three days later Pankhurst made her first public speech at an open-air meeting. More windows were broken, including those at this hall. This time Pankhurst and a group of Suffragettes went to prison.

From then until the outbreak of war in August 1914, Sylvia Pankhurst was arrested eight times. In jail, she would go on hunger strike until her dangerous condition meant she had to be released on compassionate grounds. Once she had recovered she could be rearrested due to a new law passed by the Liberal government derided as the 'Cat and Mouse Act'. Sylvia mocked it in her own way. Released, she organised a public meeting at Bromley Hall in 1914. Police were massed at the back. As soon as she started speaking they stormed towards the stage as supporters shouted 'Run, Sylvia, run!' She was out the back quicker than the cops and off in a hay cart to Epping Forest.

Address Bromley Public Hall, Bow Road, Bow E3 3AA | Getting there Underground to Bow Road (District and Hammersmith & City lines); Bow Church DLR; bus 8, 25 or 108 | Hours Mon–Fri 9am–4.30pm, closed every second Wednesday of the month | Tip Most of Sylvia Pankhurst's East End sites have since been demolished, but at 45 Norman Grove, a mile or so to the north-west, the Suffragettes ran their toy factory providing work and gifts for local women. To mark the centenary, in 2014, the residents threw a Suffragette period street party.

91 Tayyab's

Love me tandoor at this legendary curry house

Tayyab's is more than a curry house. It's an addictive way of life. Which is why the queues stretch along Fieldgate Street, a back street between the Blind Beggar pub and the East London Mosque. But don't fret, the queues move with graceful gastronomic contemplation. Tayyab's came third in a recent Yelp Top 100 eateries list, Yelp using ratings given by ordinary people, rather than restaurant critics. But when it comes to restaurant critics, as Jay Rayner once explained, there are two things worth eating here – all of its meat and all of its breads.

For many years, there were four food outlets here: at one end was the original Tayyab's, which opened in 1972 when curry was still a novelty locally. Alongside was a café, an Indian sweet shop, and at the end New Tayyab's, created out of a converted pub, hostelries starting to go out of fashion in the area. Old Tayyab's and New Tayyab's both served the same menu. When one closed at 5pm, the staff moved to the other Tayyab's. The confusion couldn't last long. Eventually the premises reopened simply as Tayyab's: one huge wide room with black marble floors and walls painted peach. Thankfully the menu was unchanged.

So, what has made this into an institution? One item on the menu: the lamb chops. They come sizzling with bountiful onions fresh from some infernal cooking machine residing in heaven, marinated to within one inch of their lives, as one wag put it, and then served on an achingly hot iron skillet. Amazingly, some punters order other things, which is a bit like going to a Led Zeppelin gig to see the warm-up act. In 2017, disaster struck. The Home Office prosecuted the owners for employing illegal immigrants. The capital wept. Thankfully the government feds saw sense, recruitment policies were tightened, and Tayyab's reopened. The best time to get there is any time. It is unlicensed but there are no corkage fees.

92 The Ten Bells

Legendary pub at the heart of the East End

Pubs are disappearing from the Brick Lane area at an alarming rate, but The Ten Bells is deservedly legendary. First of all, it sits in a highly conspicuous position on Commercial Street, in drinking-up distance from the Georgian gorgeousness of Fournier Street, the bustle of Spitalfields Market and the sacred glory of Christ Church. Indeed, the pub is named after the bells from the famed Hawksmoor church opposite.

The Ten Bells is compact and old fashioned. There is a mural of painted tiles on the wall entitled *Spitalfields in ye Olden Time – visiting a Weaver's Shop* and a new mural, *Spitalfields in Modern Times*, featuring, inevitably, illustrious neighbours Gilbert and George. On occasional Saturday nights, there is an interesting disco.

In the 1880s, Jamie Oliver's great-great-grandfather was landlord. Around the same time the pub was popular with the local prostitutes. So even more exciting is the story of how at least two of the prostitutes who were victims of Jack the Ripper – Annie Chapman and Mary Kelly – and their friends definitely drank here, a story backed up with historical evidence. Indeed, some sources say Kelly, the last victim, picked up her clients outside.

The pub has changed its name many times over the years. In 1755, it was known as the Eight Bells Alehouse. When the church installed a new set of chimes, it had to become the Ten Bells. Later the number of bells was increased to 12, but Ten Bells stayed … until the 1980s when during the centenary of the Ripper in a controversial populist move it temporarily became the inevitable 'Jack the Ripper' – until the women's group, Reclaim the Night, campaigned to convince the brewery that a murderer of women should not be commemorated so. The pub features in the remarkable 2001 Ripper film *From Hell*, a scene showing Inspector Abberline, played by Johnny Depp, having a drink with Mary Kelly.

Address 84 Commercial Street, Spitalfields E1 6LY | Getting there Underground (Circle, Central and Hammersmith & City lines) and National Rail to Liverpool Street; bus 242 | Hours Sun–Wed noon–midnight, Thu–Sat noon–1am | Tip The nearby Golden Heart at 110 Commercial Street, built in the 1930s and now listed, used to be the toast of the art world. Tracey Emin who was based locally and used to drink there gifted artefacts.

93__ Thames Ironworks

Shipbuilding colossus that once ruled the waves

Thames Ironworks was one of the world's greatest engineering and shipbuilding companies, occupying both banks of the River Lea, where it meets the Thames, at the furthest reach of the East End. Founded in 1837, the year Victoria became queen, the company was soon employing so many workers that ferries would take them from one bank to the other.

Thames Ironworks provided the metal for Isambard Kingdom Brunel's bridge over the River Tamar Devon–Cornwall border in the 1850s. But mostly the firm made ships, such as HMS *Warrior*, ordered by the Admiralty. When launched in 1860 it was the world's largest warship. Thames Ironworks even made similar ships for foreign governments, such as Prussia, Romania and Portugal. By the end of the century, the works was being run by philanthropist Arnold Hills, a teetotal vegetarian and virulent anti-smoker. Hills opposed trade unions. During a strike in 1891 his workmen hissed him as he entered the yard. Nevertheless, he set up a 'Good Fellowship' scheme of bonuses and reduced the working day to eight hours. This was mostly so that employees could spend their time on recreational activities, for Hills was obsessed with sport. Thames Ironworks had clubs for cycling, cricket and football. Indeed, the works football team has lasted much longer than the works, going on to become one of the country's best-known clubs – West Ham United – cup winners of Europe in 1965.

Disaster struck on 21 June, 1898 with the launch of the Admiralty's *Albion*. After three failed attempts, the vessel finally hit the water but created a huge wave that poured over the bridge, destroying it, and throwing spectators into the river. Thirty-seven people died. The company collapsed just before World War I, unable to compete with yards on the Tyne and Clyde, despite petitioning Winston Churchill, First Lord of the Admiralty, for help.

Address Orchard Place, The Orchard, Poplar E14 0JW | Getting there Bus D3 | Hours Accessible 24 hours | Tip At the very end of the East End is the Orchard (see ch. 64), with its lighthouse, strange container flats, American diner and general tumbleweed feeling of the forgotten land.

94 Three Mills Island

Of renovated mills and film studios

In what is almost an island, surrounded by the River Lea and its peculiarly named tributaries, are two mills with strange conical roofs, all that remains of what was one of London's oldest industrial estates.

Three Mills Island is an oasis of graceful Georgian elegance in an area blighted by a fearsome motorway and an excess of railway lines, now home to one of Britain's leading television and film studios. In mediaeval times, the land was owned by Stratford Langthorne Abbey, whose Cistercian monks tamed the water with artificial walls, compacting mud with their bare feet. By the 17th century there were as many as nine mills here. They made gunpowder, produced flour for the bakers of Stratford-atte-Bowe, refined sugar and ground grain that could be used in the alcohol industry. Peter Lefevre, a Huguenot refugee, bought the site in the 1720s. In 1872, Nicholson gin distillers took over. Following damage caused in World War II, Bass Charrington stepped in. Here was bottled that staple spirit of bad 1970s' discos, Bacardi. There was also sugar refining in the part now redeveloped as Sugar House Island for business and living.

The area later took on its modern-day name once the nine had been reduced to three. Now only two remain, the windmill having gone, and the wheels no longer turn. These are Clock Mill, rebuilt 1815–17, and House Mill from 1776, the largest surviving tide-powered mill in Britain, and some say in the world.

A campaign in the 1970s saved the site. Media companies, keen on an obscure location away from prying eyes, moved in. Films produced here include *Lock, Stock and Two Smoking Barrels* (1998) and *28 Days Later* (2002). Television programmes include *Footballers' Wives*, *Brick Lane*, *The Mighty Boosh*, *Prime Suspect* and *Big Brother*. It was also the location of the Big Brother house from the early series, since demolished.

Address Three Mill Lane, Bromley-by-Bow E3 3DU | **Getting there** Underground to Bromley-by-Bow (District and Hammersmith & City lines) | **Hours** Site accessible 24 hours; mill tours Sun May–Oct 11am–4pm; Mar, Apr & Dec first Sunday of the month |**Tip** Spend an afternoon exploring the local waterways that snake around these edgelands between the eastern end of the East End and what used to be quaintly referred to as 'London Essex'.

95 Tower Hill Executions

Hundreds put to death at infamous punishment spot

With thousands pouring out of Tower Hill tube every hour to make for the Tower itself, it is easy to miss the site of what was one of London's main mediaeval execution locations, a square pattern in stone in front of Trinity House, to the west of Tower Hill tube station.

For Simon Sudbury, Archbishop of Canterbury, who in 1381 became one of the first to be killed here, it wasn't even an official punishment. He was dragged out of the Tower of London by the mob during the Peasants' Revolt, the guards turning a blind eye. Tempers were already inflamed in the East End after King Richard II had met the rebel leaders at Mile End (see ch. 65). At Tower Hill he was beheaded after eight blows to the neck.

The most famous execution to take place here was that of Sir Thomas More on 6 July, 1535. He had been found guilty of high treason after refusing to support Henry VIII's divorce from Catherine of Aragon. In 1685, the notoriously unreliable executioner Jack Ketch tried to execute James Scott, 1st Duke of Monmouth, an illegitimate son of Charles II, who had staged an abortive attempt to seize the throne. On mounting the scaffold, Monmouth, hoping to guarantee a clean cut, handed the executioner six guineas. His first blow made only a slight wound. Even after a second attempt the duke's head refused to budge. Eventually the executioner finished him off with a knife. Later, the authorities realised they had no official portrait of the duke, so the royal surgeons stitched his head back on and tied a white cravat around his neck to make him look more appealing to the portraitist.

The last person to be executed here was Simon Fraser, Lord Lovat, on 9 April, 1747. Lovat was a Jacobite, a supporter of those who wanted the Stuarts back on the throne. He had been charged with treason. But it was more than Lovat who died. The viewing platform collapsed and 20 people were killed.

Address Tower Hill, Tower Liberty, EC3N 2NR | Getting there Underground to Tower Hill (Circle and District lines) | Hours Accessible 24 hours | Tip Britain's most famous tourist attraction can be found to the south, on the other side of the busy main road. If you don't have the time to take in The Tower of London there's usually something of interest going on by its moat.

96 Toynbee Hall

Charity central to creating the Welfare State

Toynbee Hall is a charitable institution aiming to bridge the gap between people of all backgrounds, and an oasis of calm in a hectic part of the East End. It was founded by Canon Samuel Barnett and his wife Henrietta on Christmas Eve 1884. When they had earlier arrived in the East End to take up a post at a local church, the Bishop of London had warned them that this was the 'worst district in London, containing a large population of Jews and thieves.' The Barnetts were pleased. That's exactly why they had moved here.

They named the institution after Oxford historian Arnold Toynbee, who had coined the phrase the 'Industrial Revolution' and believed that the free market system disadvantaged the poor. He had died in 1883. A descendant is the modern-day left-wing journalist Polly Toynbee. Toynbee Hall was designed in an Elizabethan style by Elijah Hoole. It sports gables, tall chimneystacks, mullioned windows and diamond-paned casements, the better to create a rustic, peaceful atmosphere.

Clever thinking also went into the interior. The dining room was set deliberately low to encourage a more convivial atmosphere. Toynbee Hall became a centre of social reform. Social workers lived in so that they were close to the poverty that then gripped Spitalfields and Aldgate nearby. An even more radical vision was that it would be a training ground for future leaders to live and work as volunteers in the East End at the coal face of poverty, and develop practical solutions they could use in national life.

It worked. Two of their social workers went on to create the welfare state, its founder William Beveridge and 1940s' Labour prime minister Clement Attlee. This remarkable history has been honoured by recent politicians. Tony Blair came to launch his campaign to end child poverty at Toynbee Hall in 1999 and David Cameron announced welfare reforms here in 2011.

Address 28 Commercial Street, Spitalfields E1 6LS | Getting there Underground to Aldgate East (District and Hammersmith & City lines); bus 242 | Hours Mon–Fri 10am–1pm & 2–4pm | Tip A few hundred yards to the west, on Old Castle Street, is the Trades Union Congress (TUC) Library, a huge repository of labour history books.

97 Traitors' Gate

The watery access to the Tower

Some of the most infamous names in English history have entered the Tower of London through this entrance as prisoners: two wives of Henry VIII, Anne Boleyn and Catherine Howard; Henry's Lord Chancellor, Thomas More; and Lady Jane Grey, the queen who never was.

Traitors' Gate was built as a water-gate entrance to the Tower. It was designed by Master James of St George for Edward I in the 1270s so that the king could now enter the Tower from the river. As the Tower came to be used more and more as a prison for those accused of treason, it took on the nickname Traitors' Gate. When prisoners were brought here they passed under London Bridge where the heads of those recently executed were displayed on pikes.

Anne Boleyn, Henry VIII's second wife, was arrested for treason, adultery and incest on 2 May, 1536, along with her brother, George, and Lord Rochford, accused of adultery with the queen. As she passed through Traitors' Gate she was met by William Kingston, the Constable of the Tower, and asked him: 'Shall I go to some dungeon?', to which Kingston replied, 'No, madam, you shall go to your chambers whereat your Grace lay before your Coronation.' Seventeen days later, after bouts of hysteria and depression, she was executed. Anne's daughter, Princess Elizabeth, the future queen, also came through Traitors' Gate. She had been arrested on the orders of the then queen, Mary, her half-sister, who had accused her of trying to usurp her powers. Elizabeth believed she would meet the same fate as her mother, and initially refused to enter, swearing she was no traitor. As it was raining she reluctantly proceeded. The case against her collapsed.

By the mid-19th century the water level had risen and so the outer archway of the gate was bricked up. The last traitor to be dealt with at the Tower was the German spy, Josef Jakobs, shot by firing squad on 15 August, 1941.

Address The Tower of London, Tower Hill EC3N 4AB | Getting there Underground to Tower Hill (Circle and District lines) | Hours Accessible 24 hours | Tip After some serious historical research about traitors and executions, raise a glass to the unfortunate at the Hung, Drawn and Quartered pub at 26 Great Tower Street.

98__Turner's Old Star

'And now for the boozer'

Pubs named after famous artists are hard to find in London. Search in vain for the Van Gogh's Ear. But Turner's Old Star, tucked away on an eerily quiet Wapping back street, has the strangest of links with that great chaser of the sun, London's greatest ever painter, J. M. W. Turner (1775–1851). Old Star is also one of the few remaining old-fashioned 'proper' East End boozers. Yes, here is a pub without craft ales that taste like washing-up liquid or artisan breads served on a spade.

Turner converted two cottages in the 1830s into a pub. It was near the site where Lydia Rogers was found guilty of being a witch in 1658. He put his mistress, Sophia Booth, a widowed landlady from Margate, in charge. As someone who often mixed in elevated company, Turner was understandably secretive about his east London wanderings and that from his twenties he kept several mistresses, who bore him four illegitimate children. When with Miss Booth he adopted *her* surname, and was known as 'Puggy Booth', a reference to his understated height and portly physique, as captured by Timothy Spall in the 2015 Turner biopic. It was only after Turner's death that a stash of his erotic drawings was discovered among his bequest. It seems they were created following weekends of drunken debauchery in Wapping. John Ruskin destroyed them to protect his charge's reputation.

The pub has been put to good use. It featured as the Pig and Whistle in the lauded 2015 Krays film *Legend* (in which Tom Hardy plays both twins) and as the setting for the infamous fight between the Krays and their even more powerful rivals, the Richardsons. One of the saddest declines in the modern-day East End is the sight of an old pub withering away or having been converted into a curry house or flats. The days when this area hummed with the vitality of the docks are gone, which only makes pubs like this even more of a find.

Address 14 Watts Street, Wapping E1W 2QG, +44 (0)203 726 5371,
www.turnersoldstar.co.uk | Getting there Overground to Wapping; bus 100 | Hours
Mon–Fri noon–11.30pm, Sat noon–late, Sun noon–evening | Tip A pub trawl south
along Wapping High Street and its continuations that hug the river can be most
rewarding, visiting the Captain Kidd, Prospect of Whitby and Town of Ramsgate.

99 University of the Ghetto

First stop for those new to the East End

Hundreds of immigrants – Jews a hundred years ago, Bangladeshis more recently – taught themselves about English ways, customs, literature, politics and life at what was Whitechapel Library, known popularly as the University of the Ghetto. In a shock move, the council closed it in 2005 and the space was subsumed into the adjacent Whitechapel Art Gallery.

The building, with its asymmetrical front and fin-de-siècle Art Nouveau touches, is itself an anomaly in this depressed part of London. The idea came from the philanthropist, publisher and Liberal MP J. Passmore Edwards who had pledged that only the best was good enough for the people. The library opened on 6 May, 1892 and soon became a refuge from overcrowded noisy houses. At home, the children of the immigrants spoke in their own indigenous languages, their parents knowing no English. At the library, they could teach themselves at what was the intellectual heart of one of the most radical and diverse communities in Britain, and it quickly built up one of the biggest collections in any library of Jewish books, overtaken, in the 1970s with books in Bengali.

In the first year, membership topped 2,500. Users' occupations ranged from diamond cutters to feather merchants, via lard refiners, presumably not Jewish. Among the hundreds of thousands who poured through its doors were the artist Mark Gertler; Jacob Bronowski, best known as the TV presenter of his own brilliant anthropological history, *The Ascent of Man*; and playwright Arnold Wesker, who captured the local ghetto in works such as *Chicken Soup and Barley* (1956). Perhaps the best description came from the playwright Bernard Kops for whom the library recalled: 'How often I went for warmth and a doze/The newspaper room whilst the world outside froze/And I took out my sardine sandwich feast/ Whitechapel Library, Aldgate East.'

Address Whitechapel Library, now Whitechapel Art Gallery, 77–82 Whitechapel High Street, Whitechapel E1 7QX | **Getting there** Underground to Aldgate East (District and Hammersmith & City lines); bus 25, 205 or 254 | **Hours** Tue–Sun 11am–6pm | **Tip** The East End is rather short on art galleries but is packed with street art. Turn round the corner to Osborne Street and head north into Brick Lane. The streets are your canvas.

100 V2 Mansions

The Nazis' last target

Hughes Mansions is a drab, forgettable 1920s' block of flats in Spitalfields. It was rebuilt after being partly destroyed by the Nazis on Tuesday 27 March, 1945 in the last attack on London during World War II. One hundred and thirty families were killed, most of them Jewish. But the story is that Hughes Mansions was deliberately targeted.

When it was built, Hughes Mansions had all mod cons, even inside toilets. What an improvement on the cramped and basic tenements that had filled the area! The war hit the East End worse than any part of London. On the night of 10/11 May, 1941, the last of the original type of air attack on London occurred when a bomb fell here. Just one person was killed. Soon the Nazis had a new weapon and it hit the East End on 13 June, 1944. It was the *Vergeltungswaffe* or reprisal weapon, the V1, a flying bomb. It landed on Grove Road, Bow, killing six people. What was so shocking was that this time the aeroplane had no pilot; *it* was the bomb. More V1s landed across London, causing major destruction. When the Allies destroyed the V1 launching pads in France, the Nazis responded with the even more destructive V2.

The attack on Hughes Mansions was no ordinary bombing. The estate was chosen for being home to so many Jews. The traitor Lord Haw-Haw boasted about the destruction on German radio, telling his many listeners that 'those dirty Jews and Cockneys will run like rabbits into their holes.' The attack on Hughes Mansions was the last on London during the war, but it was not the last attack *within* Hughes Mansions. On the 60th anniversary of the atrocity in March 2005 a commemoration organised by a local Jewish group was marred when those attending, mostly elderly, were pelted with food, eggs and flour from hoodlums high up on the decks. The police refused to investigate for fear of upsetting the Bangladeshi community.

Address Vallance Road, Spitalfields E1 5BJ | Getting there Underground (District and Hammersmith & City lines) and Overground to Whitechapel; bus D 3 | Hours Accessible 24 hours | Tip One Jewish phenomenon they couldn't wipe out here is Rinkoff's, a super-lative bakery at 79 Vallance Road.

101_ Victoria 'People's' Park
The East End's back garden

The East End's biggest park acts as a buffer between Tower Hamlets and the residential suburbs of Hackney to the north. It was landscaped by Sir James Pennethorne in 1842, a time when the rapid expansion in the population meant that green space was vital.

The park is a day out in itself as there are so many delights. Of most interest are the Dogs of Alcibiades statues, the Burdett-Coutts Fountain and two stone alcoves from the original London Bridge. The Dogs of Alcibiades guard the park just north of Sewardstone Road. The name is a slight misnomer. Usually, as at the British Museum, there is only dog. The legend dates from a story, *Life of Alcibiades*, by the Greek biographer Plutarch. Alcibiades was a 5th-century BC Athenian statesman and tergiversator who owned a large, handsome dog but cut off his tail to gain pity from the locals he was oppressing.

The Burdett-Coutts Fountain is a magnificent 1862 Gothic shrine in pink marble, granite and stone. It was commissioned by Angela Burdett-Coutts, the richest woman in the Victorian East End, and features four clock faces, pointed arches, sculpted cherubs and inscriptions. More importantly, it provided clean water to people whose memories of cholera was fresh. The park's most unusual feature, *pace* those dogs, are pieces of old London Bridge. They stand three metres tall and are older than the park itself, dating back to the 1760s. David Copperfield reveals that they are his favourite place to sit in the Dickens novel of the same name. Two other alcoves have survived, one at Guy's Hospital in Southwark and the other in East Sheen.

To music fans, the park is fondly remembered as the setting for one of the most important gigs in London history, organised by Rock Against Racism on 30 April, 1978. Forty-two coaches came just from Glasgow. Headlining were the dynamic Tom Robinson Band and the Clash at their peak.

Address Stretching from south Hackney in the west to the motorway at the east | Getting there Overground to Hackney Wick or Cambridge Heath; bus 277 or 425 | Hours Daily 7am to dusk | Tip Head east along the Hertford Union Canal to the even more massive, 21st-century Queen Elizabeth Olympic Park, home of the 2012 Olympics.

102— Viktor Wynd Museum of Curiosities

The entire strangeness of the world in a basement

Curios, arcana, esoterica, weirdities, extraordinary ephemera. This is more than a museum, it is a trip into another world. Officially the Viktor Wynd Museum of Curiosities, Fine Art & Natural History, this little-known gem opened in 2014 in what seems a wilfully perverse setting: the drab, weather-beaten edgelands where Bethnal Green meets Hackney.

The idea for this mausoleum of madness came from the Last Tuesday Society, founded in 1873 at Harvard University and brought to London in 2006. The Society is dedicated to 'subverting life, the universe and everything bored of the life and world it sees around. It seeks to create a new world filled with beauty, wonder and the imagination.' The museum's aim is to present an incoherent vision of the world within a tiny space, and so there is no attempt made at classification and comprehensiveness, or as it explains 'to show the world not in a grain of sand, but in a Hackney basement.'

That has certainly happened here. On entering, a sign warns: *Those easily offended by death and decay should stay away – over 21s only – no poor people.* It's appropriate advice. On show are two-headed lambs, shrunken heads, tribal skulls, dead babies in bottles, the skeleton of a giant anteater, condoms used by the Rolling Stones and parts of pickled prostitutes. Every available surface has been crammed with stuff, from bones of the dodo to armadillo handbags to an enormous ball of hair removed from a cow's stomach. On the staircase hangs a collection of stuffed game – hartebeest, warthog, eland – animals not usually seen in east London.

The venture follows a long-standing east London tradition for bizarre establishments: similar strangeness was on show at Charlie Brown's long-gone and still mourned pub in Limehouse.

Address 11 Mare Street, Hackney E8 4RP, +44 (0)207 998 3617, www.thelasttuesdaysociety.org |
Getting there Overground to Cambridge Heath; bus 26, 106, 254, 388 or D6 | Hours
Wed – Sat noon – 11pm, Sun noon – 10pm; there is a bar serving cocktails, and London's only
L'Heure Verte (Absinthe Hour) every weekday 6 – 7pm | Tip Head half a mile north-west to the
revitalised and vibrant Victorian Broadway Market.

103 _ Virginia Settlers' Plaque

Remembering the founders of Jamestown, Virginia

A large stone plaque honours the brave souls who left the East End on 20 December, 1606 to found Jamestown in Virginia. The trip was organised by the Virginia Company, which had received a charter from James I. They sailed in three ships: the *Susan Constant*, the *Godspeed*, and the *Discovery*. On board the ships were 39 sailors, and 105 men and boys.

In charge was Captain Newport who had been instructed to find a location that was safe from Spanish marauders. He found what is now Chesapeake Bay, sailed up a river he named the James, and located 50 miles inland a low-lying peninsula to set up home – Jamestown – named after the king. It was the first permanent English settlement in North America. Virginia, the state, had been named after the king's predecessor, Elizabeth, the virgin queen.

At first the settlers found hospitality from the natives and created a colony. But within a year they had succumbed to diseases from the swampy land, exacerbated by the typhoid and dysentery they had brought with them. It took some time to recover.

The Virginia Settlers were not the only pioneers to the New World to leave from this part of the Thames. The Pilgrim Fathers sailed in the *Mayflower* from Rotherhithe on the southern bank. Although this East End location, traditionally Brunswick Wharf, is now eerily quiet, during the great days of the docks this was where thousands of ships were built or repaired, just east of a bend by the Isle of Dogs that was ideal for anchorage.

Originally, the plaque was fixed to the wall of Brunswick House and unveiled in 1928. Following World War II damage, Brunswick House was demolished. The now free-standing memorial was vandalised, its bronze mermaid stolen. Brunswick Wharf collapsed into imperceptibility when the docks closed but recent gentrification has made it safer and more secure. The renovated memorial was unveiled in 1999.

VIRGINIA QUAY

THIS VIRGINIA SETTLERS MEMORIAL TABLET WAS
PART OF THE WALL OF
BRUNSWICK HOUSE WHICH FORMERLY STOOD
ABOUT 180 YARDS NORTH WEST OF THIS POINT
IN 1999, BARRATT HOMES LIMITED REINSTATED
THIS MONUMENT AND COMMISSIONED
THE PLANISPHERIC ASTROLABE
BY WENDY TAYLOR CBE

Address Thames Path, off Jamestown Way, Blackwall E14 2DE | Getting there East
India DLR | Hours Accessible 24 hours | Tip Have a wander around the nearby streets
where the names are reminders of the area's past (Adventurers' Court, Susan Constant
Court, Pilgrim Mews …).

104 Wall of Heroes

Tributes to the heroes of the Left

On the wall of this obscure sited alleyway where Aldgate meets Whitechapel is a gallery of socialist heroes featuring the philosopher Noam Chomsky and the anarchist Peter Kropotkin. It was created by Freedom Books, the long-standing left-wing publishers and bookshop based here.

Freedom Books was established after World War II by Vernon Richards as an HQ for editing the anarchist paper *Freedom*. Richards' real name was Vero Recchioni. He was the son of the Soho deli owner Emidio Recchioni who once tried to assassinate Italian fascist dictator Benito Mussolini. Richards was imprisoned in 1945 for conspiring to cause disaffection among members of the armed forces.

Anarchism used to be big business in the East End, especially early in the 20th century, when the German Rudolf Rocker was campaigning locally. Rocker found horror in the East End. He was disturbed by the sight of the poor, who 'went about in foul rags through which their skin showed, dirty and lousy, scavenging their food out of dustbins and the refuse heaps that were left behind after the market closed.' He launched the anarchist newspaper *Der Arbeter Fraint*, which was written in Yiddish, even though he was a gentile.

After a group of anarchists were burned out of their hideaway on Whitechapel's Sidney Street in 1911, the press discovered anarchism. But rather than disappear from the East End, the anarchists were emboldened. They organised a successful and much talked about tailors' strike in 1912. Walking through Whitechapel one day, Rocker was stopped by an old Jew with a long white beard who greeted him: 'May God bless you! You helped my children in their need. You are not a Jew, but you are a *mensch*.'

In Victorian times Angel Alley was where the local prostitutes, including some of those associated with the Jack the Ripper murders of 1888, plied their trade.

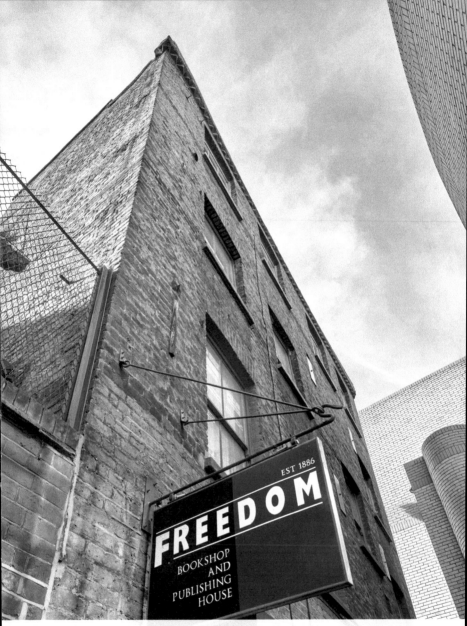

Address Angel Alley (leading to Freedom Bookshop), off Whitechapel High Street, White-chapel E1 7QX | Getting there Underground to Aldgate East (District and Hammersmith & City lines); bus 25, 205 or 254 | Hours Accessible 24 hours | Tip A welcome green space can be found just up the high street close to Whitechapel tube station. Vallance Gardens was a Quaker Burial Ground from 1687 to 1857, and later laid out as a public garden in 1880 after the social reformer Henrietta Barnett saw the need for poor local families to have somewhere to relax.

105 — The Wapping Tunnel
World's oldest underwater tunnel

There are hundreds of tube tunnels in London but nothing like the Wapping Tunnel. Deep below the street at Wapping station, this is the oldest river tunnel in the world and now takes trains 400 yards to and from Rotherhithe.

The tunnel's engineers were the revered father and son team of the Frenchman Marc Isambard Brunel and the better-known Isambard Kingdom Brunel. Marc Brunel began work on the tunnel in 1825. He devised an ingenious digging technique from watching a shipworm burrow. It led to the workmen digging inside a protective frame while bricklayers built the wall as they advanced. The technique has been used for every major tunnel built since. Funding for the scheme came from luminaries such as the Duke of Wellington, but when the monies dried up the project was abandoned for seven years. It was eventually finished in 1843 by son Isambard Kingdom Brunel.

It was back-breaking work and hazards were everywhere. Raw sewage seeped in. There was the ever-present threat of fire from methane gas. Thames water broke in to flood the tunnel five times. On 12 January, 1828, the waters broke through. Isambard Brunel was trapped under a fallen beam but managed to tear himself free. He ran for his life only to be caught in the water, which bore him along and spat him out onto dry land. Six men drowned that day.

On the tunnel's first day, 25 March, 1843, some 50,000 people took the staircase down at Wapping, paying a penny to walk through. In the first three months, a million people used the tunnel, which was said to be the most visited tourist attraction in the world. Eventually the novelty wore off. It became a haunt of prostitutes and was sold to the railways, becoming part of the London Underground system in 1865 on the then somewhat obscure East London line. Although underground, just to confuse matters the line is now known as the Overground.

Address Wapping Station, Wapping High Street, Wapping E1W 3PA | Getting there
Overground to Wapping; bus 100 | Hours Only when the trains are running | Tip Forgo
the subterranean world to take the Thames Path east, heading towards Canary Wharf for
the immense riverine views and feeling of freedom away from the bustle of the street.

106 West India Docks

Where the fruits of a thousand isles were unloaded

West India Docks still survive, although the confectionous contents of the Caribbean are no longer unloaded here. The three parallel stretches of water occupy over 164 acres at the north-west end of the Isle of Dogs. The docks were opened on 21 August, 1802 by the prime minister, William Pitt. The West India Dock Company had gained a 21-year monopoly for importing vital goods from the West Indies: rum, coffee and sugar.

It was the sugar that caused the most trouble. So dangerous was the handling of sacks that the landing stage water was streaked with blood from the men's hands. The loss of a finger in the bight was an occupational hazard. The presence of such much-wanted cargo tempted a thousand miscreants, and so riverside security here was intense; scores of men armed with pistols and swords, which simply led to ever more ingenious scams. Three dockers leaving a gate unsteadily turned out to be two men and a pig's carcass dressed in a shabby suit and battered hat. A team of robbers distracted a shipmaster, broke into his office and emptied an entire barrel of sugar, slipping the contents into bags and passing them out through the window. A man leaving the docks was stopped by an official who remarked: 'You feel rather lumpy, my man,' to which the man replied: 'That's my lunch!' 'Well, just step in here a minute.' A quick search revealed two bottles of brandy hidden in the man's clothing.

To Joseph Conrad, the greatest of all maritime novelists, 'In the New South Dock there was no time for remorse, introspection, repentance … From six in the morning till six at night … the great slings of general cargo swinging over the rail, to drop plumb into the hatchways at the sign of the gangway-tender's hand.' When the Docks closed in 1980 the most remarkable waterside regeneration in England began, with the old docks an exciting feature of the new Canary Wharf.

Address South of Hertsmere Road, E14 4AL | Getting there West India Quay DLR; bus 135, 277, D3, D7 or D 8 | Hours Accessible 24 hours | Tip To the north of these docks is the free Museum of London Docklands, open daily 10am–6pm. It's also worth looking at the intensely and cumbersomely worded plaque on Hertsmere Road set on one of the few surviving dock walls.

107 Where Stalin Met Lenin

Dictators once lodged at the 'Monster Doss House'

In 1907, they were just a group of noisy, strange-looking, bearded Russians – Bolsheviks – in London for a political conference, as nowhere else would have them. History has been kind to them – in some places – for their number included Joseph Dzhugashvili and Vladimir Ilyich Ulyanov, better known by their dictator names, Joseph Stalin and V. I. Lenin. Also in attendance was their equally influential and revolutionary cohort, once revered, later vilified: Leon Trotsky.

They came to London by train, arriving at Liverpool Street station, where they were met by the English Friends of the [1905] Russian Revolution, which included James Ramsay MacDonald who became Labour's first prime minister some 20 years later. The English Friends had laid on a dinner for the foreign dignitaries but were surprised to discover that the Russians had not brought with them – wait for it – their dinner suits. None of them owned such bourgeois mufti or even knew what dinner suits were.

The communists met at the Jewish socialist club on the corner of Fulborne Street and Whitechapel Road, now a sari shop. Lenin sorted out everyone's rooms. He ensured Stalin stayed in some discomfort here at Tower House, a fearsome-looking structure, which the American writer Jack London had decried as 'the Monster Doss House.' In one cubicle slept Maxim Litvinov who later became the Bolsheviks' representative in London at the time of the Russian Revolution, as well as Soviet ambassador to Washington. Also staying here were Lev Kamenev and Grigori Zinoviev. They and Stalin became the three most powerful figures in Russia on the death of Lenin in 1924 – until Stalin ordered their executions during the show trials of the 1930s.

The 'Monster Doss House' is now a block of flats. It was built by Lord Rowton, Disraeli's secretary, as one of a series of upmarket lodging houses for the penniless in 1902.

Address 81 Fieldgate Street, Whitechapel E1 1GU | **Getting there** Underground (District and Hammersmith & City lines) and Overground to Whitechapel | **Hours** Viewable from the outside only | **Tip** Head west along Fieldgate Street if only to see just the outside of the now closed down – temporarily, it is hoped – Whitechapel Bell Foundry, with its elegant period façade, where the later cracked Liberty Bell of Pennsylvania was cast.

108 William Gladstone's Red Hands

Blood spilled during bitter trade union dispute

The hands on the statue of William Gladstone, one of Britain's greatest prime ministers, have been streaked red to symbolise the blood the women trickled onto the statue during an infamous late 19th-century industrial dispute.

In 1888, some 1,500 female workers at Bow's Bryant & May match factory went on strike over pay and conditions in what is now seen as one of the most significant events in English labour history. The match girls were working with dangerous yellow phosphorus that caused a whitening of the skin and loss of hair. Worse still, their jaw withered away and the face discharged a foul pus in a form of bone cancer that often caused an early death. Many firms had banned yellow phosphorus, but not Bryant & May.

The women were working a 14-hour day, their already low wages exacerbated by fines levied for talking, dropping matches or having bare feet. The girls were even forced to help fund a statue of William Gladstone, the political hero of the factory owner, Theodore H. Bryant. When he closed the factory to 'celebrate' the unveiling of the statue, some of the women cut their arms and let the blood trickle onto the statue, which they said they had paid for metaphorically with their blood.

The strike began on 5 July, 1888 after the owners tried to force the girls to sign a statement about how well they were being treated. The journalist and women's rights activist Annie Besant lobbied her well-connected friends to boycott Bryant & May matches. A deputation of the match girls marched on Fleet Street and Parliament. Three weeks later the company announced it would rehire the sacked workers and end the fines system. The strikers had won an unexpected victory! Ten years later Bryant & May stopped using yellow phosphorus.

Address By Bow Church, 230 Bow Road, Bow E3 3AH | Getting there Bow Church DLR | Hours Accessible 24 hours | Tip Head north-east to the former match girls' factory at 60 Fairfield Road that has long been converted into the Bow Quarter apartments.

109 William Kent Arch

Remnant of grand London mansion saved and moved

One of the most surprising and incongruous sights in the East End is this grand Classical-styled 18th-century arch fronting a community centre in run-down Bromley-by-Bow.

The arch was designed by the lauded architect William Kent and was rescued from Northumberland House, the immense London residence of the Percy family, the last of the great houses in Charing Cross to go. Its demolition by order of the Metropolitan Water Board, to build Victoria Embankment in 1874, shocked London.

The arch was rescued and first moved to the garden of Tudor House in St Leonard's Street, Bow. When London County Council chose to demolish Tudor House and turn the gardens into a public park, the arch was off again, to here. Given that few East End buildings have been designed by a major architect, the William Kent arch is something special. William Kent (1685–1748) was a leading architect in early Georgian Britain. He introduced the Palladian style of architecture into the country and devised a new style of landscape gardening. In Rome, he met the Earl of Burlington, one of the leading architectural patrons in England. The earl took him back to London to decorate Burlington House in Piccadilly, where Kent lived for the rest of his life. One of his most famous works is Horse Guards Parade on Whitehall. Not everything he did was universally accepted. Robert Adam criticised Kent's works as 'immeasurably ponderous.'

Bromley-by-Bow, the area around this folly, is run down. Though it has a rich history, its historic buildings have long gone. The area is not helped by the urban blight and thunderous roads on coming out of the tube station.

Other relics from Northumberland House can be found in London. A lion, more than 6 metres long and 1.5 metres high, is now in Syon House near Brentford, while an interior wall can be found in the Victoria and Albert Museum.

Address St Leonard's Street, Bromley-by-Bow E3 3BS | **Getting there** Underground to Bromley-by-Bow (District and Hammersmith & City lines); Bow Church DLR; bus 488 or D 8 | **Hours** Accessible 24 hours | **Tip** Although almost everything in Bromley was wiped out by wartime bombing and motorway building, a remarkable few hours can be spent wandering the area with an old OS map, comparing and contrasting.

110 Wilton's Music Hall

Legendary venue in once bohemian now shabby square

Behind battered doors that look like they forgot to be painted lies one of London's last authentic Victorian music halls. Wilton's opened on 28 March, 1859 in rooms dating back to the 1690s. Although hard to believe now, given the urban blight all around, the now barely noticeable Wellclose Square next to Wilton's was *the* East End address to have in Georgian London, created after the Great Fire of London by Freemasons to attract intellectuals and bohemians, and later the home of Scandinavian embassies.

When John Wilton bought the business in the 1850s he refurbished in great taste, installing mirrors, chandeliers and decorative paintwork. The bill included madrigals and arias, as well as more prosaic entertainment. The leading entertainers of the day performed here. Charles Coborn's 'Two Lovely Black Eyes', which made grown men weep with laughter, achieved the impossible: it captured Bethnal Green in lyrical form. Gus Elen chanted 'A Nice Quiet Day', a story that all hard-working folk with a skeleton in the family cupboard could relate to: 'There was me and the missus and the 'arf dozen kids/Wiv nuffink in the bottle but the bung/But I gave the kids a treat/When we got to Newgate Street/'Cause I showed 'em where their uncle, 'e was 'ung.'

A fire in 1877 ruined Wilton's handiwork, but it was rebuilt to look like its previous incarnation. During the 20th century, music hall faded. With the similar demise of Wellclose Square it looked like the building might go. However, in 1966 it was acquired by the Greater London Council and saved, thanks to a campaign involving the poet laureate John Betjeman. When Fiona Shaw presented T. S. Eliot's *Wasteland* in the winter of 1997 there was no heating, which perfectly suited the intended mood. The flyer advised those attending to 'dress warmly' and one journalist added 'wear hard hats.' The venue is now more comfortable.

Address 1 Graces Alley, Whitechapel E1 8JB, +44 (0)207 702 2789, www.wiltons.org.uk |
Getting there Underground to Tower Hill (District and Circle lines); Tower Gateway DLR |
Hours Mahogany Bar: Mon–Sat 5–11pm, Cocktail Bar: Tue–Sat 6–11pm; for show
times visit the website | Tip In the centre of Wellclose Square is a school that replaced the
chapel where, according to one of the most bizarre royal history stories, Prince Eddy, Queen
Victoria's disgraced son, who died young, illegally married a Catholic shop girl in the 1880s.

111　York Hall

The East End's hardest-hitting venue

Boxing has long been one of the East End's populist pleasures, and nowhere more than at Bethnal Green's York Hall, described by many as the spiritual home of British boxing.

The famed venue opened in 1929, taking its name from the royals who presided over the official opening – the Duke and Duchess of York – who later became George VI and the Queen Mother. York Hall was originally meant for bathing. It had slipper baths and public laundry facilities. In the basement was a Turkish bath, or *banya*, enthusiastically patronised by the local Russian and Polish second-generation Jews. In the 1950s the first-class pool fell into disuse. It was around this time that York Hall started hosting boxing events. The Kray twins, who were London champions before they became full-time gangsters, sparred here. Reggie Kray even promoted all-in wrestling at York Hall.

There have been so many legendary bouts. In 1968, Des Rea won the newly created British light welterweight title here. When Nigel Benn beat American Robbie Sims on 3 April, 1991 it was the first time the American, half-brother of the legendary Marvin Hagler, had been stopped. How apt that Benn's son, Conor, was fighting here in 2019. In 1995, Joe Calzaghe took down Frank Minton in only 85 seconds. Lennox Lewis, in his early days, sent Liverpool's Noel Quarless on to his back in two in 1990. David Haye made his debut aged 22 here in December 2002, beating Tony Booth who had 121 fights to his name.

In 2003, it looked like the great referee in the Town Hall was going to call time on the venue. There were rumours that it would be converted into expensive flats. Outrage followed, and a huge campaign saw York Hall saved. The venue was redeveloped and upmarketed. The baths are now a spa, but the pugilists still pack a punch and the crowd, said to be the most knowledgeable in England, is defiantly shouty.

Address 5 Old Ford Road, Bethnal Green E2 9PJ, +44 (0)208 980 2243, www.better.org.uk | Getting there Underground to Bethnal Green (Central line); bus 106, 254, 388, D 3 or D 6 | Hours Mon–Fri 7am–9.30pm, Sat 8am–8.30pm, Sun 8am–7.30pm | Tip It was fitting that the venue would start to host boxing. Bethnal Green has a long history of fighting. Daniel Mendoza, the English heavyweight champion 1792–1795, lived a glove's throw away at 3 Paradise Row, Bethnal Green, for over 30 years. A blue plaque marks the spot.

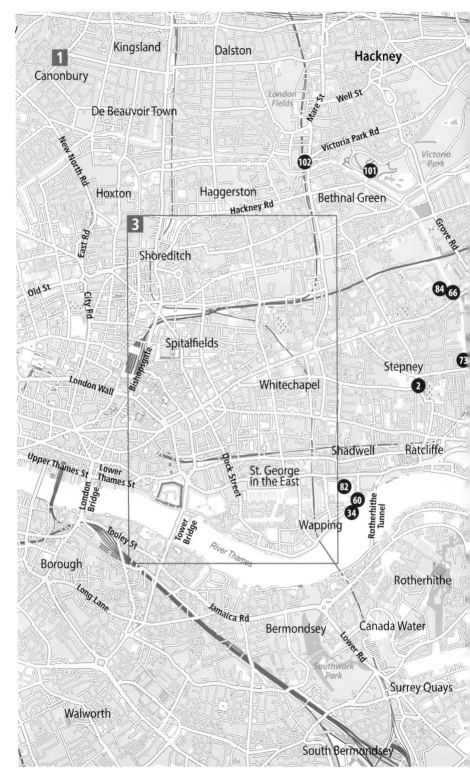

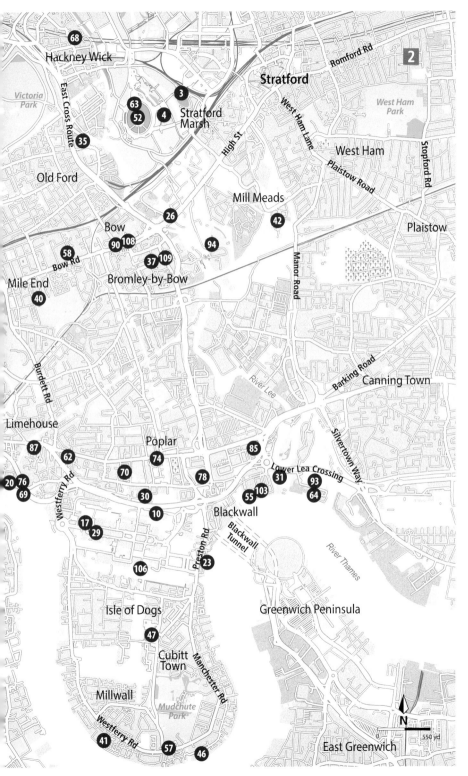

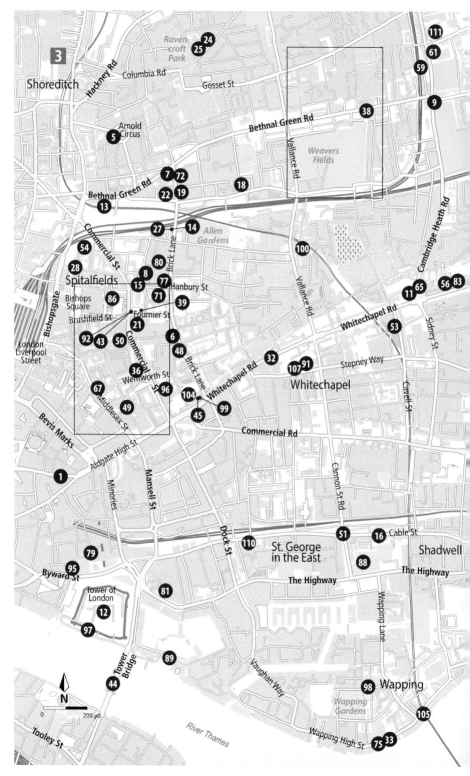

John Sykes, Birgit Weber
111 Places in London
That You Shouldn't Miss
ISBN 978-3-95451-346-8

Kirstin von Glasow
111 Coffeeshops in London
That You Must Not Miss
ISBN 978-3-95451-614-8

Nicola Perry, Daniel Reiter
33 Walks in London
That You Shouldn't Miss
ISBN 978-3-95451-886-9

Kirstin von Glasow
111 Gardens in London
That You Shouldn't Miss
ISBN 978-3-7408-0143-4

Laura Richards, Jamie Newson
111 London Pubs and Bars
That You Shouldn't Miss
ISBN 978-3-7408-0021-5

Julian Treuherz, Peter de Figueiredo
111 Places in Manchester
That You Shouldn't Miss
ISBN 978-3-7408-0753-5

Katherine Bebo, Oliver Smith
111 Places in Poole
That You Shouldn't Miss
ISBN 978-3-7408-0598-2

Solange Berchemin
111 Places in the Lake District
That You Shouldn't Miss
ISBN 978-3-7408-0378-0

Alexandra Loske
111 Places in Brighton and
Lewes That You Shouldn't Miss
ISBN 978-3-7408-0255-4

Tom Shields, Gillian Tait
111 Places in Glasgow
That You Shouldn't Miss
ISBN 978-3-7408-0256-1

Michael Glover, Richard Anderson
111 Places in Sheffield
That You Shouldn't Miss
ISBN 978-3-7408-0022-2

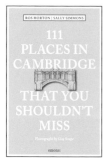

Rosalind Horton,
Sally Simmons, Guy Snape
111 Places in Cambridge
That You Shouldn't Miss
ISBN 978-3-7408-0147-2